Return to Vietnam

by Ken Palmrose

Return to Vietnam

Crossroads Publishing, LLC

620-204-1710

ISBN: 979-8-9905820-5-7

Cover Design by Author Ken Palmrose

Photography by Author Ken Palmrose

Edited by Elizabeth Morquecho

Advanced Layout and Design by Tonya Andrews, Crossroads Publishing, LLC

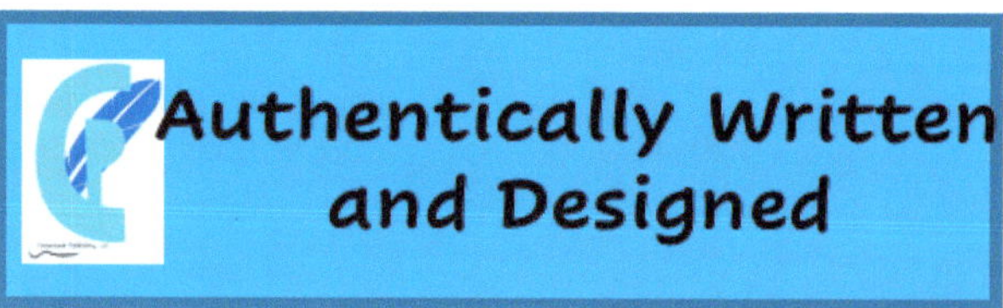

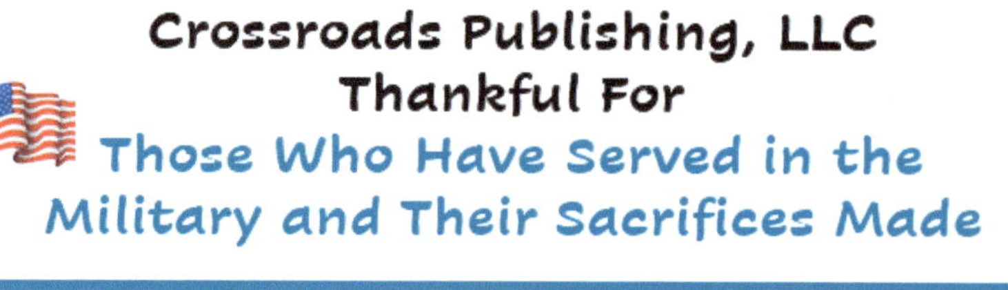

Table of Contents

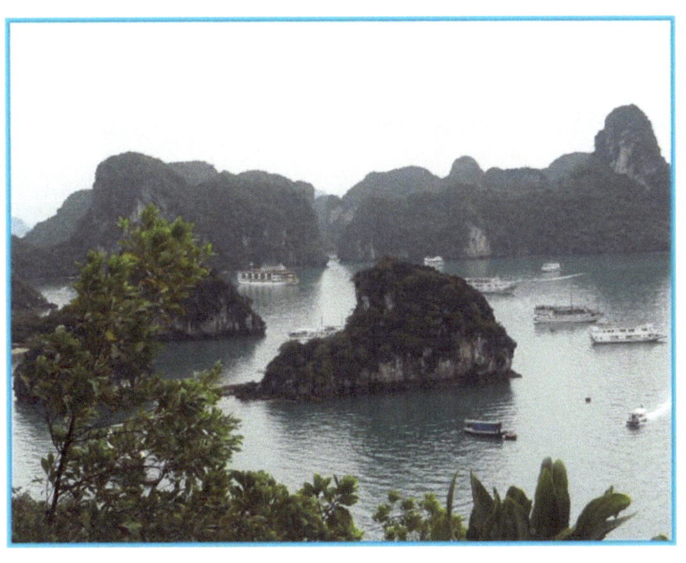

Preface

This is the story of my journey back to Vietnam many decades after my first time there in 1967-68. I was not visiting for some type of "healing" process but, rather, as part of a countrywide tour, like millions of other tourists. I went to Vietnam on a small group tour. There were three other Vietnam Vets in the group, and all four of us were back in Vietnam merely as tourists, not as veterans of America's war in Vietnam seeking something different. This journey is not a war story. I will only mention my time there during the war as a reference or comparison to what I saw so many decades ago.

Visiting Vietnam is not something many Veterans would ever do but, perhaps, some will look at this book, the photos, and anecdotes, and feel a little differently about how they view Vietnam. If not, I hope they enjoy the photos.

Vietnam is a safe country for traveling. English is spoken almost everywhere—sometimes fluently, other times not—but communicating is never an issue. Like in all communist countries, discretion is a must when discussing anything that can be deemed sensitive. Tour directors, guides, and locals will warn you if cameras and microphones are present. If you have a question that needs to be deferred, they will usually explain when and where a discussion can be continued. These continuations can be quite candid and informative.

Vietnam is a backpacker's paradise with numerous hostels located throughout the country. Many young travelers, including several women we talked with, said they had no issues traveling, whether alone or in groups. Since one can find affordable preferences via online searches, I will not be recommending hotels or restaurants. Most tours stay in nice three or four -star hotels—some higher—and, depending on the tour company you book with, you may find that you are right in the middle of historic and main sites of interest.

1 — Hanoi-The Beginning

Our journey will generally be from north to south, beginning in Hanoi. Hanoi is the capital of Vietnam, withover eight million people in the metropolitan area and is over 2,000 years old. Situated in the Red River Delta, the city is less than 60 miles from the ocean. There are hundreds of temples and pagodas to see, as well as beautiful historic buildings, including French architecture and design. There are parks, night markets and, my favorite, food. At every night market, and on every street corner, fantastic food vendors can be found.

Outside of our hotel in Hanoi, there was a school. During drop-off and pick-up times of the day, we could look out the windows and watch as families traveled by motorbikes to leave or retrieve their children—thousands of them at one time.

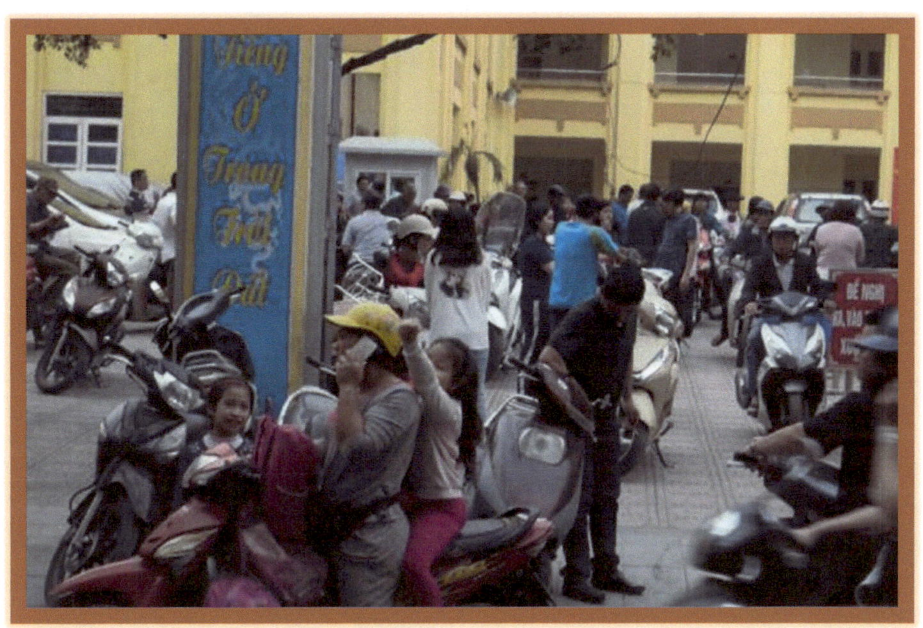

As seen in the school photo, most Vietnamese wear Western-style clothes. But I remember from fifty-some years ago that most young ladies wore the traditional *ao dai*, which was a long tunic-style top, split at the waist and covering a pair of loose-fitting silk pants. Back then, they were mostly black and white, at least where I was. Today, the *ao dai,* which is the national dress of Vietnam, is mainly seen at festive occasions and family gatherings. *Ao dai* translates to "long shirt." During my recent visit to Vietnam, the colorful versions of the national dress could be seen all over the country, while the old, conservative, black-and-white versions were seldom seen.

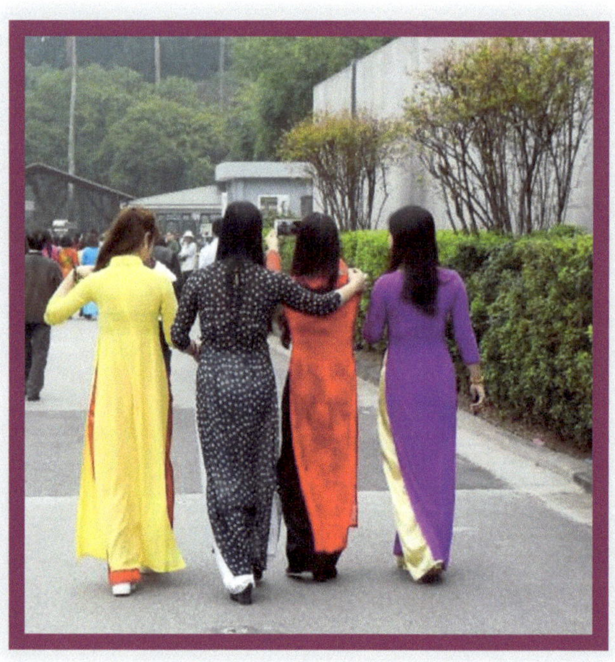

These young ladies are on their way to see the mausoleum of Ho Chi Minh, whose remains are pre-served under glass and are viewed by tens of thousands every year. Pictures are forbidden, but I can testify that it was a weird sight.

He was an amazing man, referred to as "Uncle Ho" by GIs and locals alike—by some, in less cordial terms than others. In the beginning, Ho Chi Minh admired the U.S., but his admiration faded when, in WWII, despite his attempts to reach out to our country, we chose the side of the French. The picture below shows part of the grounds around Ho Chi Minh's mausoleum, where he lived and worked.

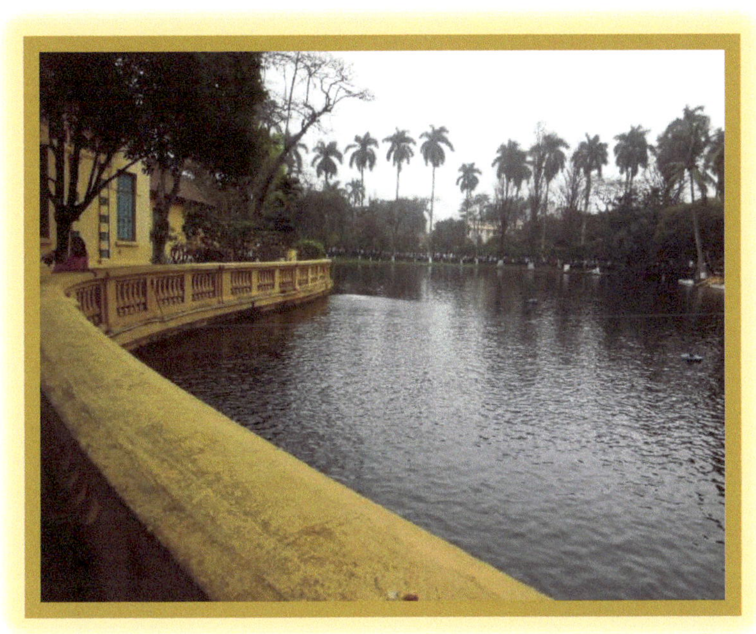

Hanoi is full of beautiful temples, parks, museums, and outstanding architecture in and around the older sections, such as the French Quarter. Before the start of our day tours, I found plenty of places to wander alone during my free time, often after enjoying an early morning coffee. During this trip, I used the app *Maps.me* on my smartphone. I only downloaded maps that covered the areas along our route, making it easy to pinpoint my hotel. The app showed the streets and alleys where I walked in real-time GPS. With my hotel pinpointed, I was not worried about getting lost while wandering the maze of alleys and streets. The app also allowed me to pinpoint specific locations where I wanted to walk to and visit. There are many such apps available for any type of smartphone.

One of the most popular sights I walked to is the Ngoc Son Buddhist Temple. The temple is on a little island and is accessed by crossing over an architecturally beautiful red bridge—a favorite picture for locals and visitors alike.

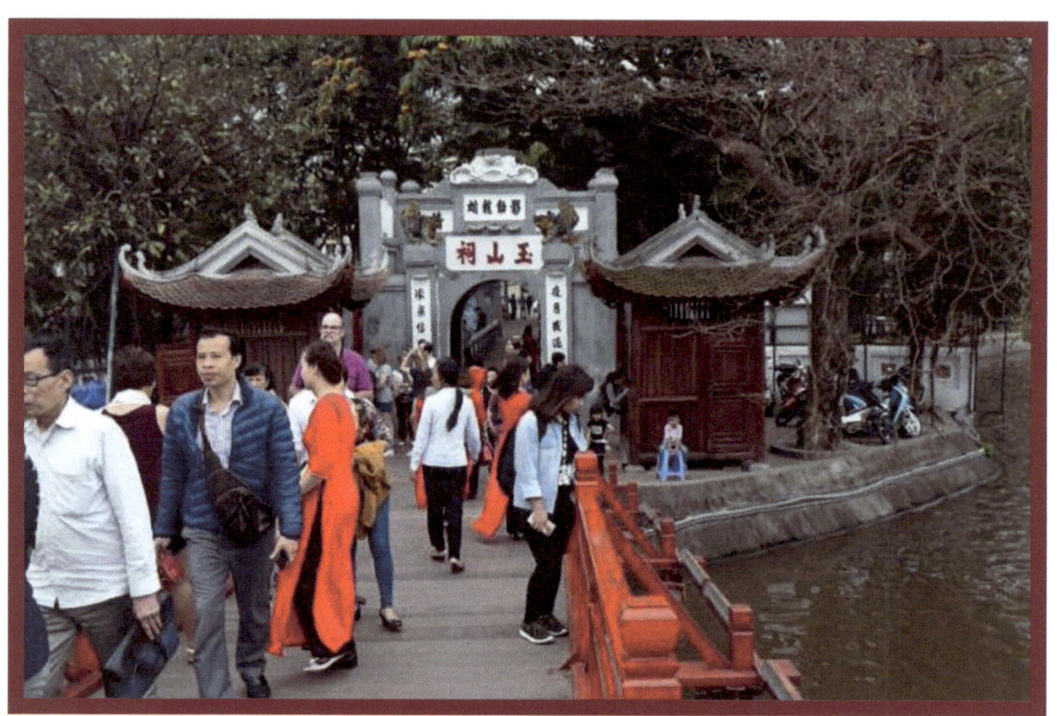

VIETNAM

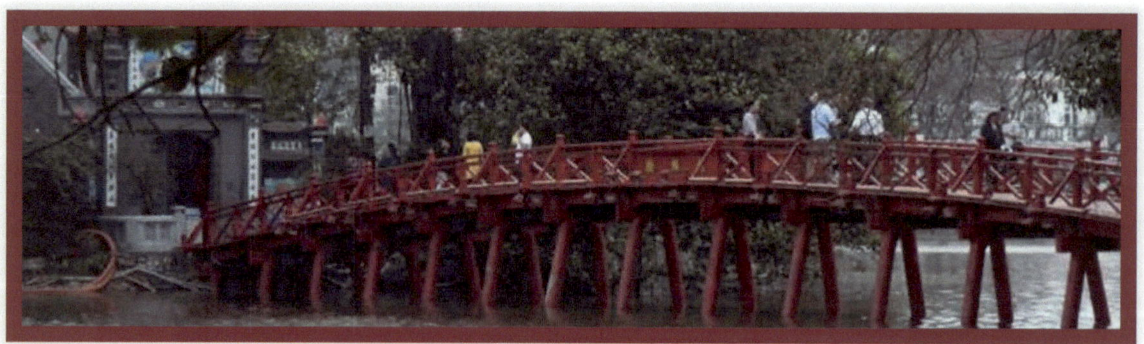

Ngoc Son is located on Hoan Kiem Lake. The lake is surrounded by beautiful parks and walkways, where thousands of people take pictures, eat with their families and friends, and the local ladies dance and exercise in numerous places around the lake. The following are just a few of the scenes from my morning walk.

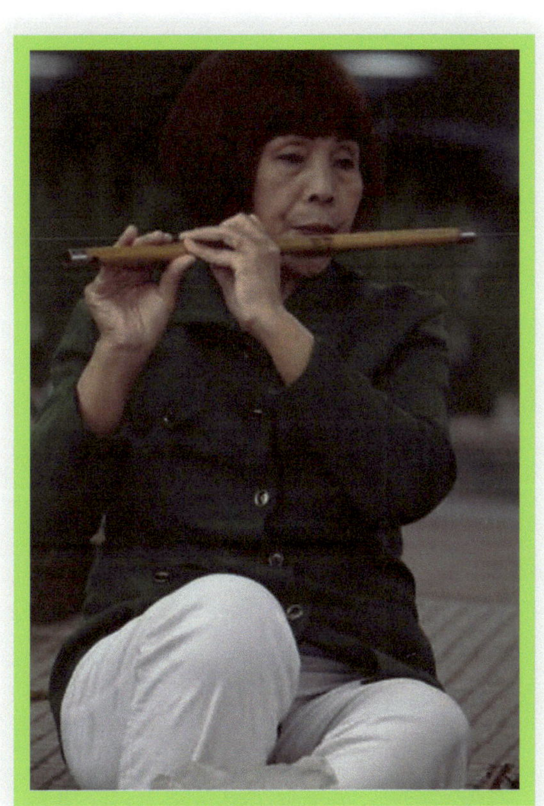

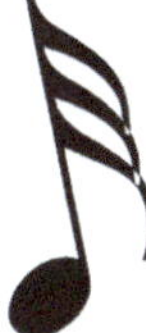

Whenever I see someone like this and wish to take their picture, I point to them and then to my camera. If they shake their head no, or otherwise indicate they do not want their picture taken, I do not take it. I have rarely been told no and have found that smiling usually helps procure a yes. The Vietnamese were more open to my picture-taking than most people from other countries I have visited.

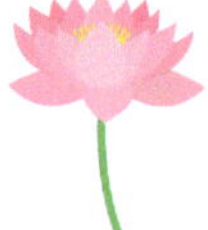

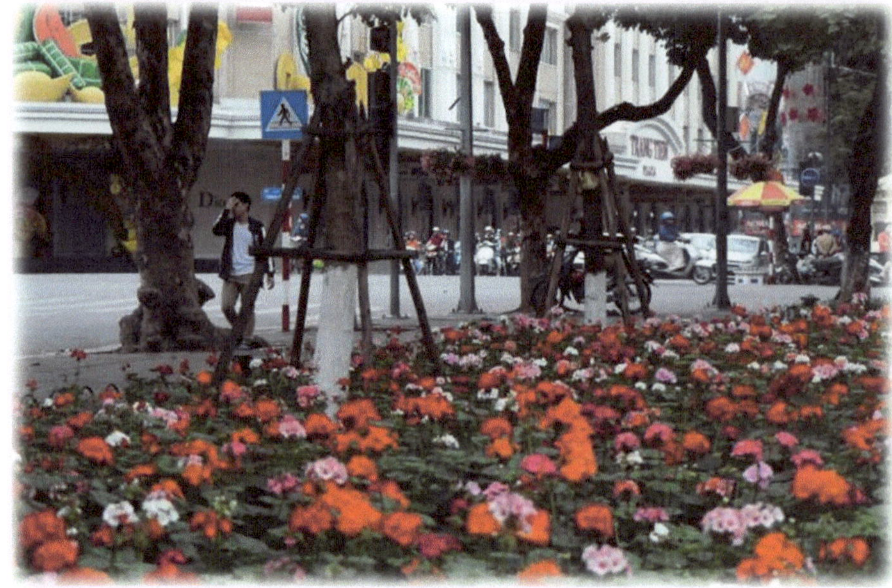

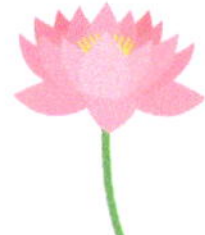

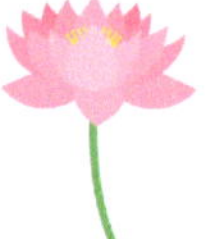

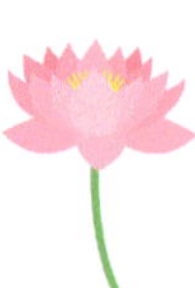

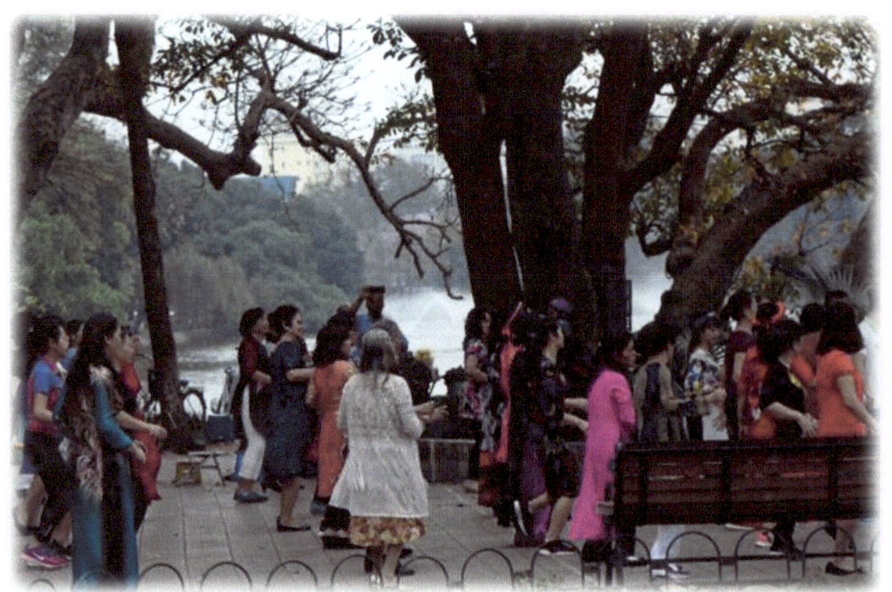

Water show puppets, both large and small, are a part of the Vietnamese culture, especially around Hanoi. Water puppetry is a unique art form in which the puppets are held out on long, slender, stick-like attachments over, and in, the water. Behind the stage, puppet masters sit halfway in the water during the entire length of the show. Water puppets have been in existence for over a thousand years, and their shows can be seen all over the country.

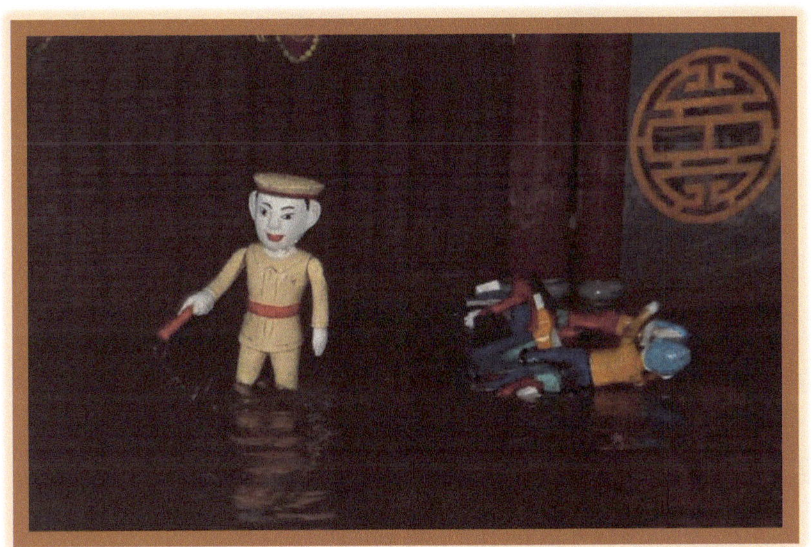

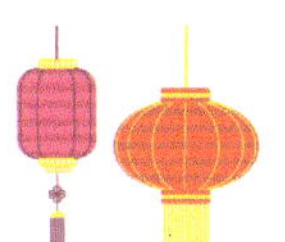

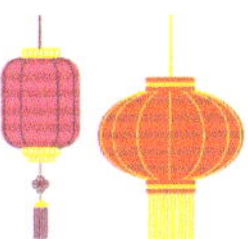

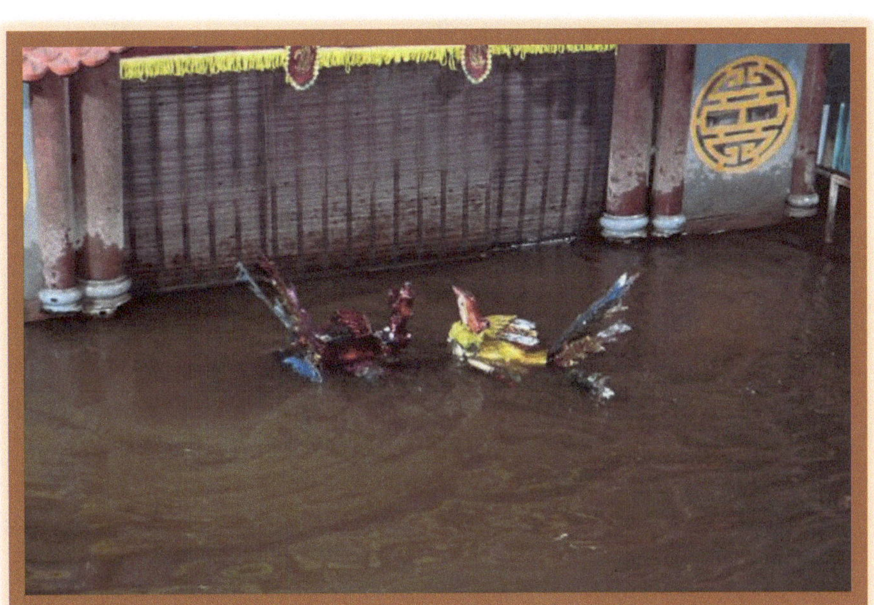

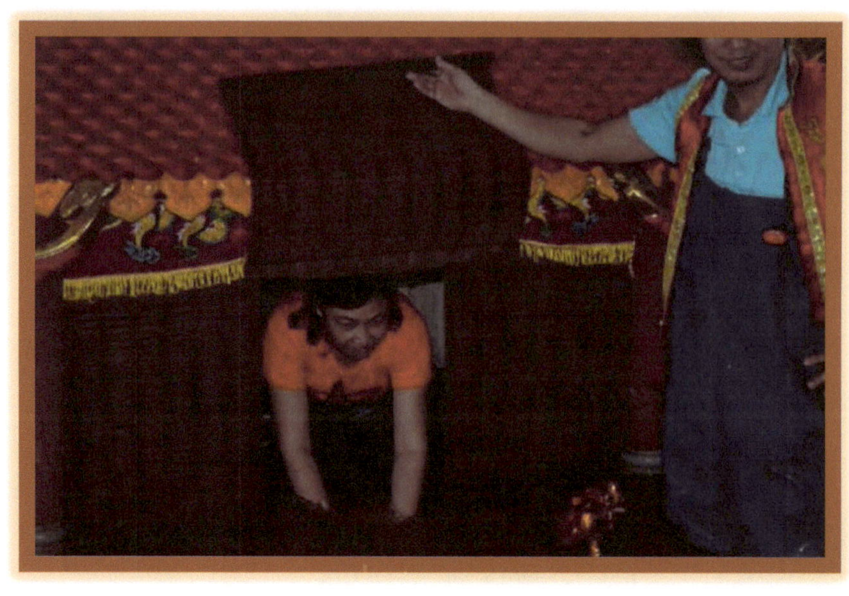

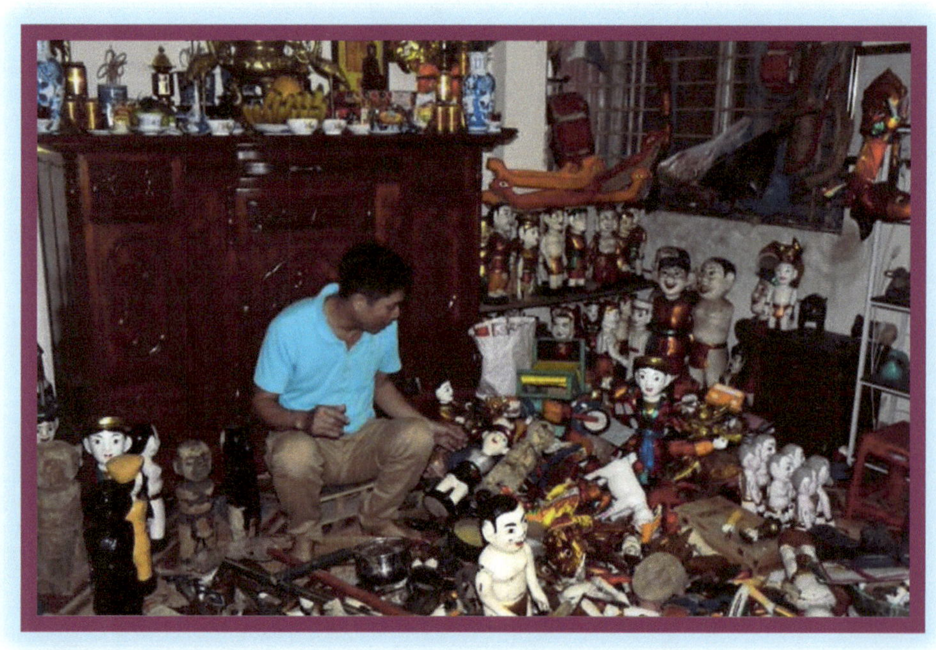

We were fortunate to have been invited to visit the home of a man who builds and repairs puppets.

One of the most interesting places to visit in Hanoi is the Vietnam Museum of Ethnology, which shows the various cultures and ethnicities throughout the country's history. The museum grounds cover more than 10 acres and include exhibits and thousands of artifacts that display Vietnam's 54 unique ethnic groups. In addition, outside the museum building, you can walk around and see exact replicas of their traditional houses and gardens, along with a wide variety of statues and carvings. I chose to spend more time here than on a tour of the infamous Hanoi Hilton, which contains too much propaganda for my taste. The educational and photo opportunities at the museum make it well worth your while.

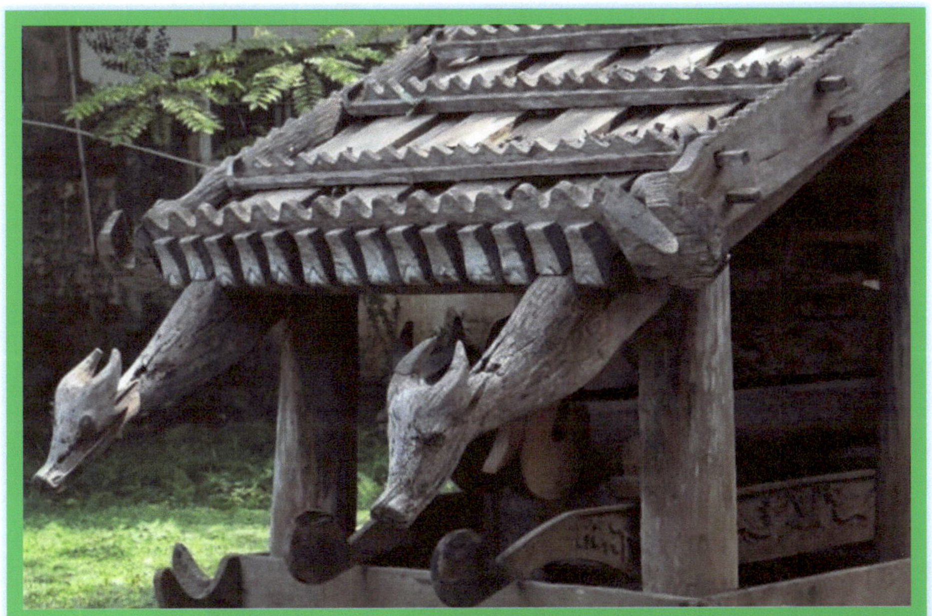

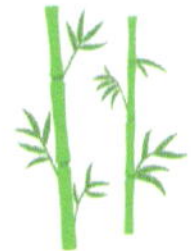

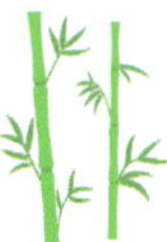

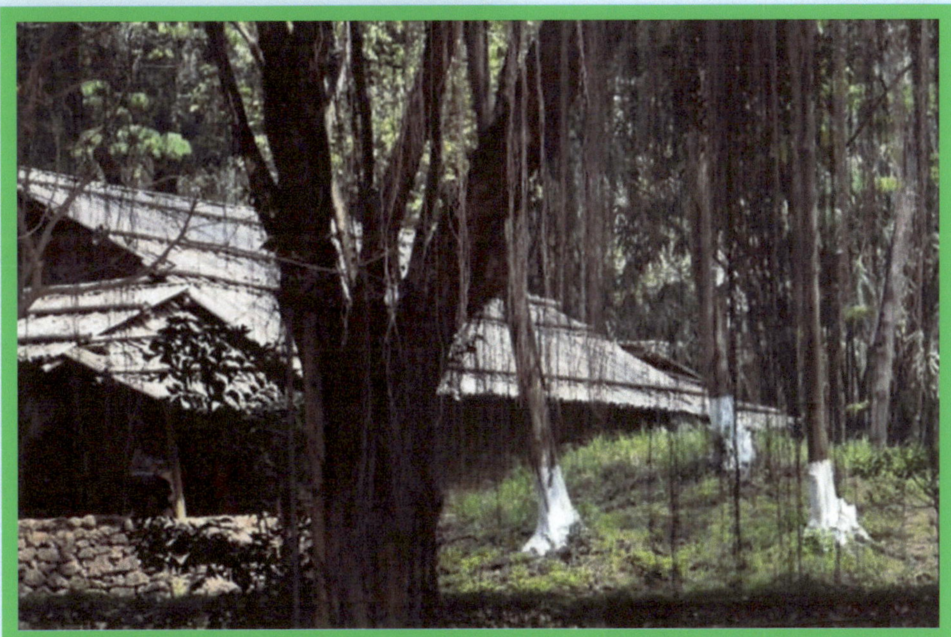

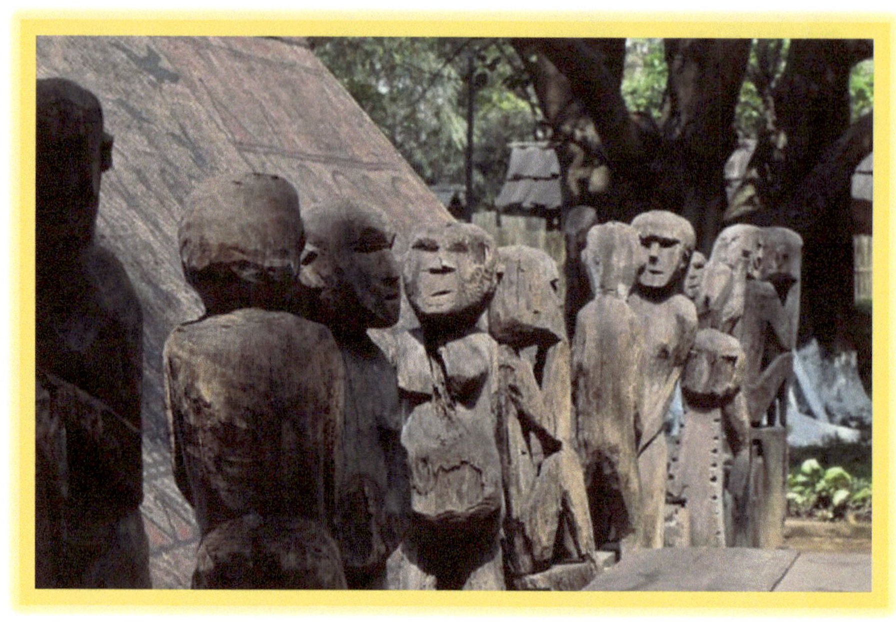

This is a good time to mention one of the things that stood out during my two-week journey: Wi-Fi. Although slow at times, it was free at every business I visited. Wherever I went to eat or drink, there was usually a card on the table with the password to access their Wi-Fi. But, as I looked up at the poles and wiring outside of each business, I found myself shaking my head in amazement that any signal could find its way to its final destination.

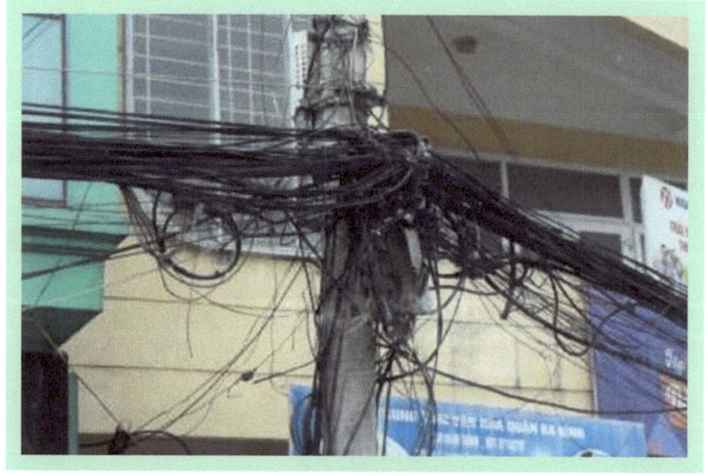

2—Getting Around

There are a wide variety of transportation types to choose from when getting around the cities, towns, and rural areas. Tuk-tuks, scooters, taxis, busses, pedicabs, bicycles, rental cars, and decent airline connections are among the modes of transportation to choose from. Tuk-tuks are found all over Asia, as well as in other countries around the world. In a major city like Hanoi or Saigon, the tuk-tuk, and other open forms of travel, are wide open to all the wonderful scents—and exhaust emissions—of a large metro area. Wherever you are using a tuk-tuk for your travel needs, you must pay close attention to their charges. I have found that, most of the time, I end up paying quite a bit less if I use a local taxi. They are generally the cheapest, fastest, and safest means around the city.

If you take a taxi and there is no meter in sight, make sure you ask for the fare first. If there is a meter, make sure it is turned on. As for renting a scooter, if you think you can safely ride in the kind of traffic you see in the next picture, go for it. I rode around Saigon and Cholon on the back of a large scooter with someone from the area; I am glad he was in control.

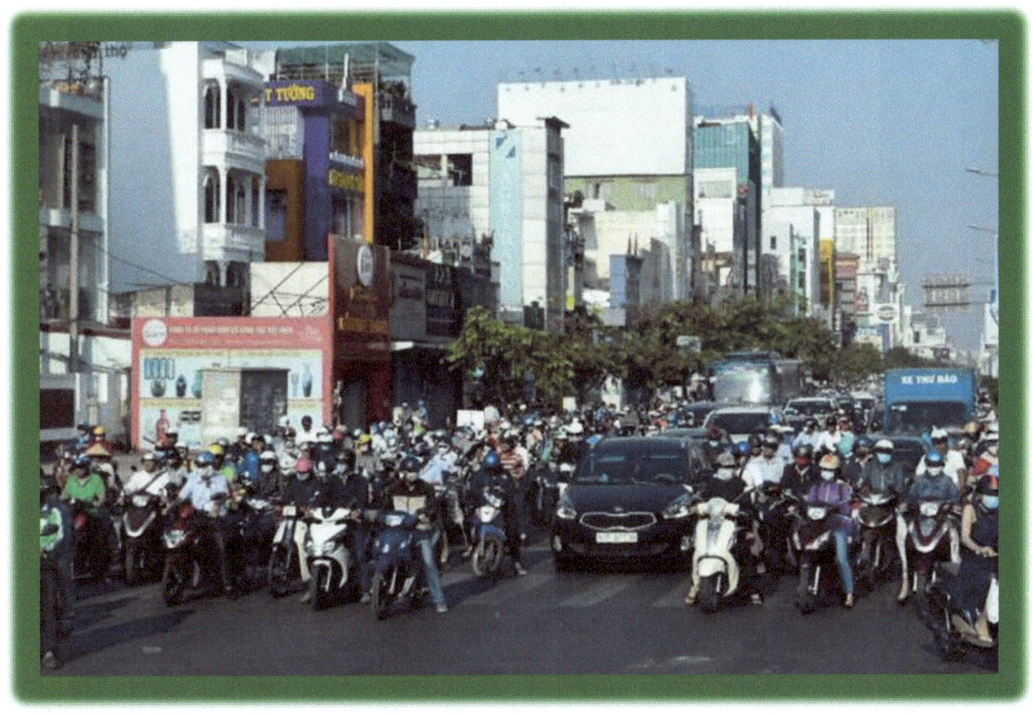

If you are familiar with operating scooters in these types of traffic conditions, there are numerous scooter rental outlets to choose from, but I prefer a taxi, like this one.

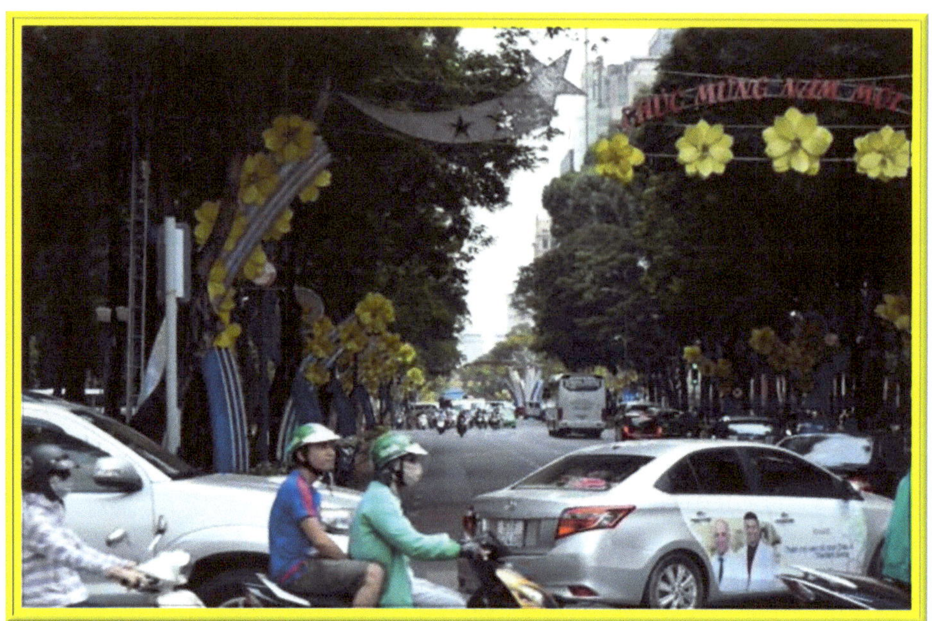

I have traveled on the water in an amazing variety of watercraft. No matter the form of travel, everyone made sure my ride was safe, whether we were in a round boat arranged by my tour or a high-powered longboat on one of the larger waterways. Riding in this round boat was one of my favorite river trips. It was a short one, but fun. There are many different types of boats from north to south—you could end up on a short ride on one or more. If you are queasy on the water, you might want to skip the round boat. The two young ladies I was riding with took great joy in making that thing go round and round in a fast circle before we headed off with the other boats in my group.

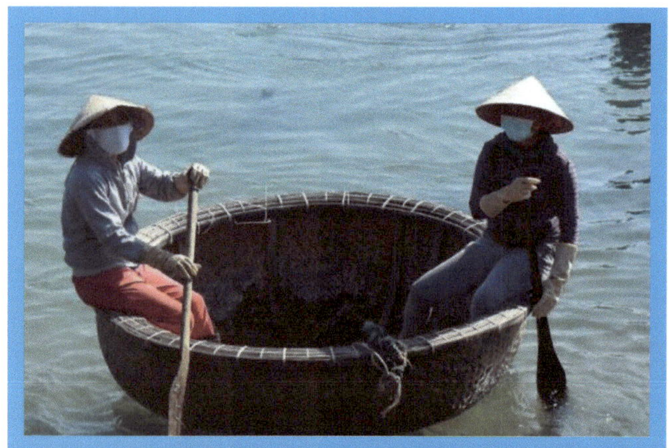

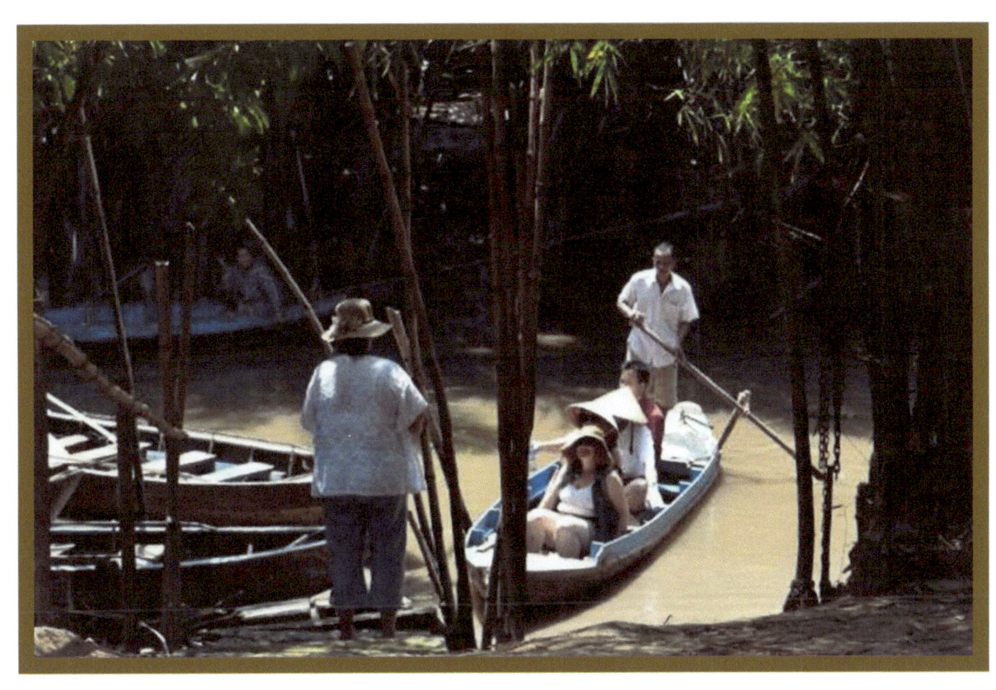

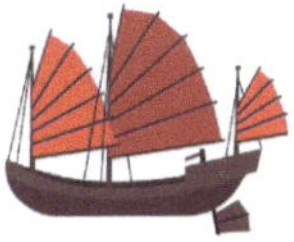

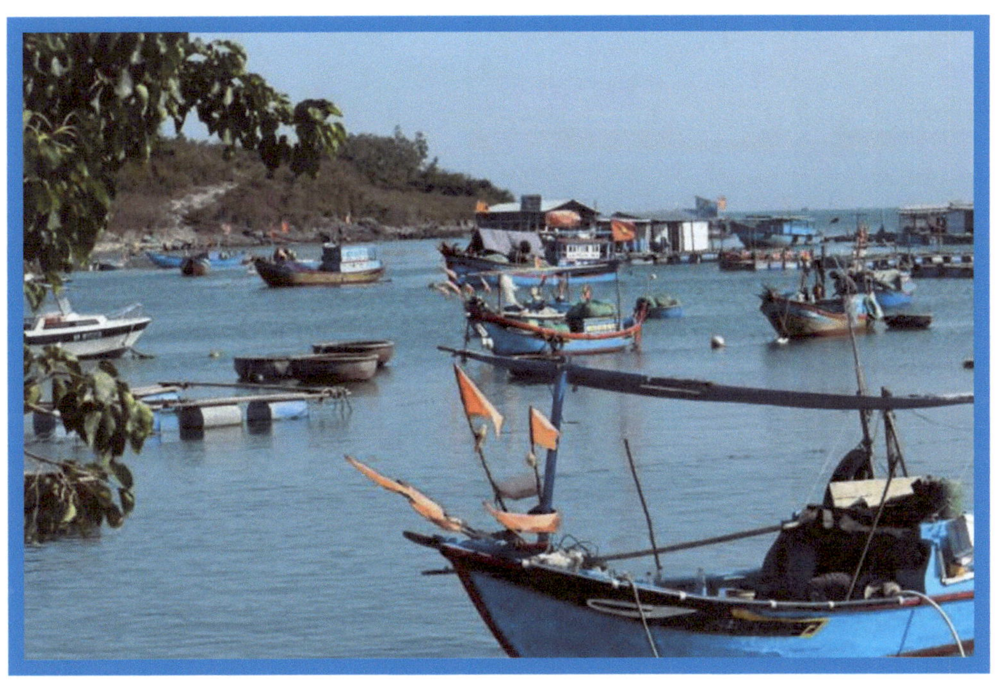

Whenever you are near the water, you will find that there are dozens of photo opportunities with all the colorful boats passing by, many with unusual and interesting designs. At times, a boat may be more than a plain old watercraft—it could be a family home.

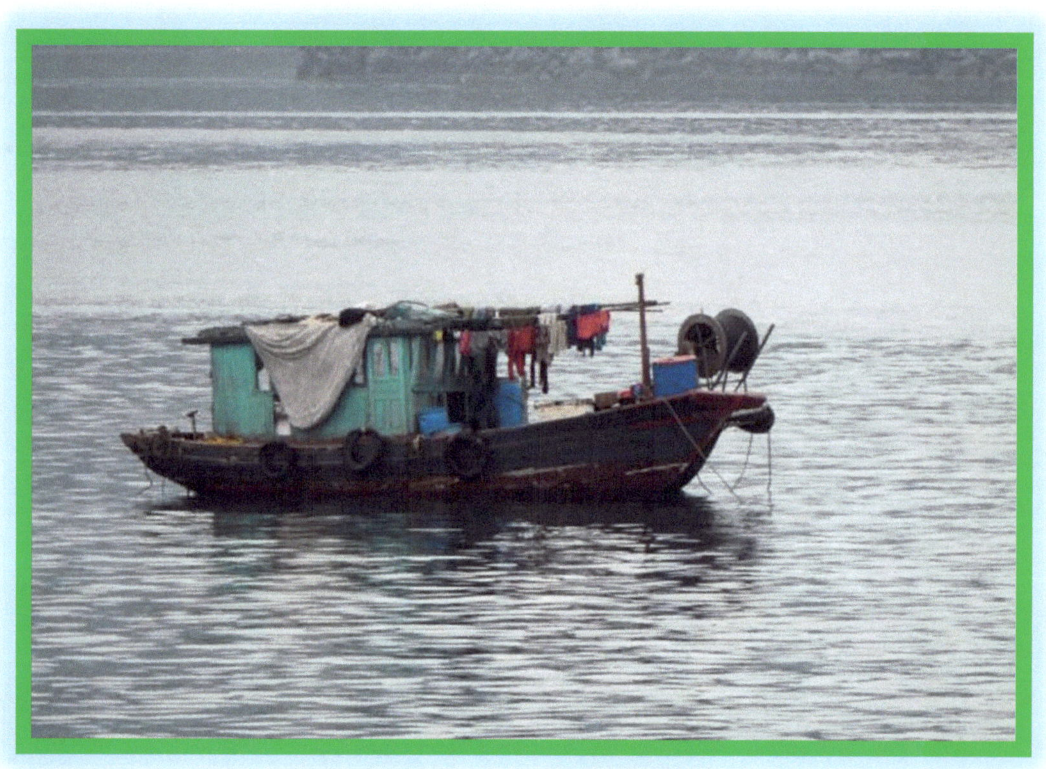

3—Ha Long Bay

Halong Bay, or Ha Long Bay, is one of the most beautiful places in all of Vietnam and, for that matter, all of southeast Asia. Most of the travel photos I have seen over the years portray this area as having beautiful blue skies and picturesque backdrops. This is a good time to inform those of you who have not yet been to this part of the world that overcast and cloudy days do occur here, many times bringing rain at any time of the year. Of course, during my visit to Halong Bay, it was cloudy! But do not let that stop you. The views and sights are still unparalleled.

The bay is known as the "Emerald Bay" and is one of the many UNESCO sites I visited on my return to Vietnam. The imposing limestone rock outcrops can be seen for miles before you get near the bay. There are hundreds of these large rocky formations rising above the water. Overcast days do not mute the beauty of Ha Long.

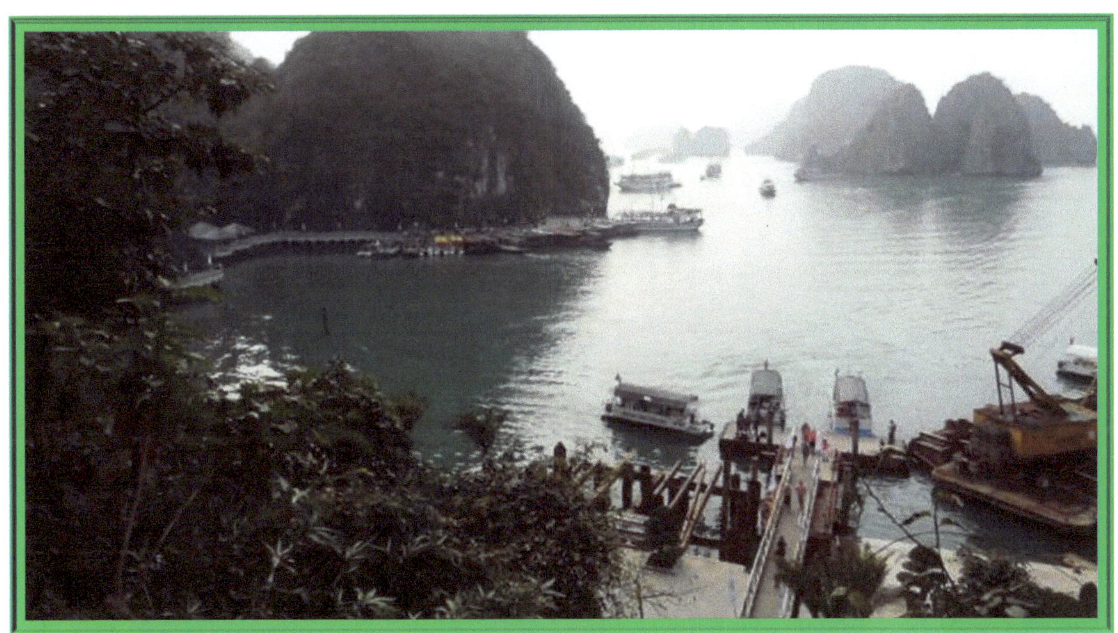

We climbed up a trail on one of the larger formations where there was a large grotto to visit as well as an outstanding viewpoint where we could see the water below, sprinkled with the different types of boats that were for overnight visitors, like us. The grotto was a big surprise to all of us who trekked up the trail and entered. It was larger than any of us had imagined.

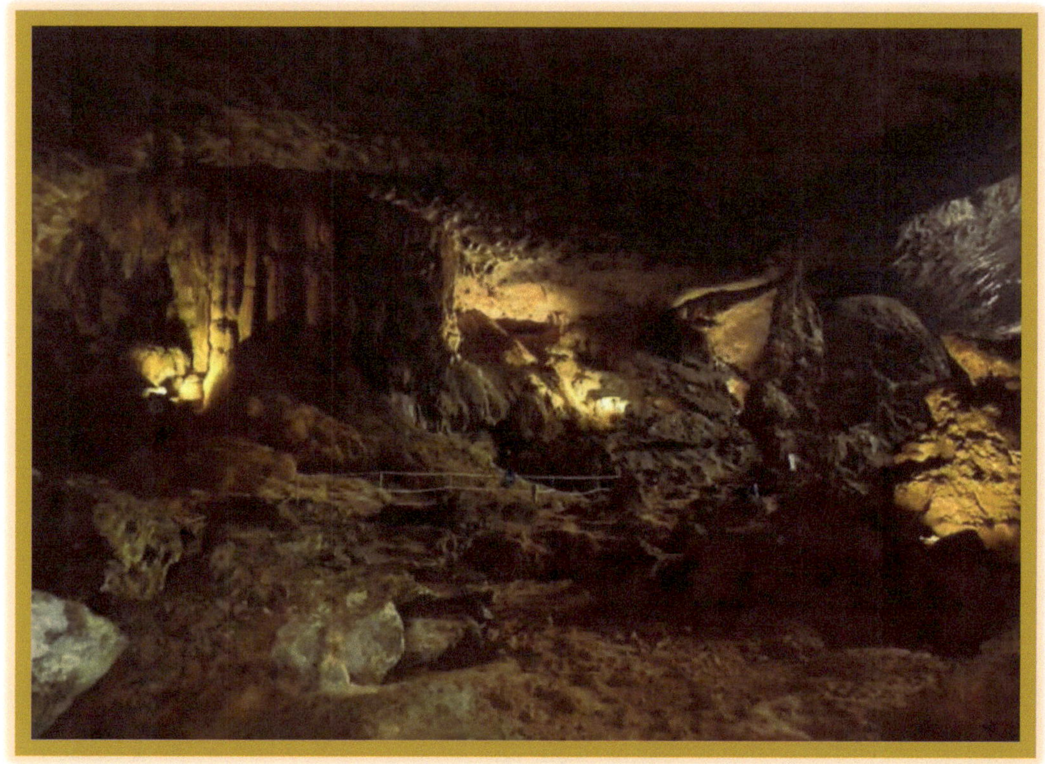

After we left the grotto, we walked around to a viewpoint where we could see a wide variety of boats on the water below. There were fishing boats everywhere, as this is a prime fishing area. Many of the family boats were the sampan style seen in movies and were powered only by oars. The view from our boat was just as spectacular at night. We could see the traditionally designed Vietnamese-style sailboats, such as the one we had spent one night aboard, off in the distance.

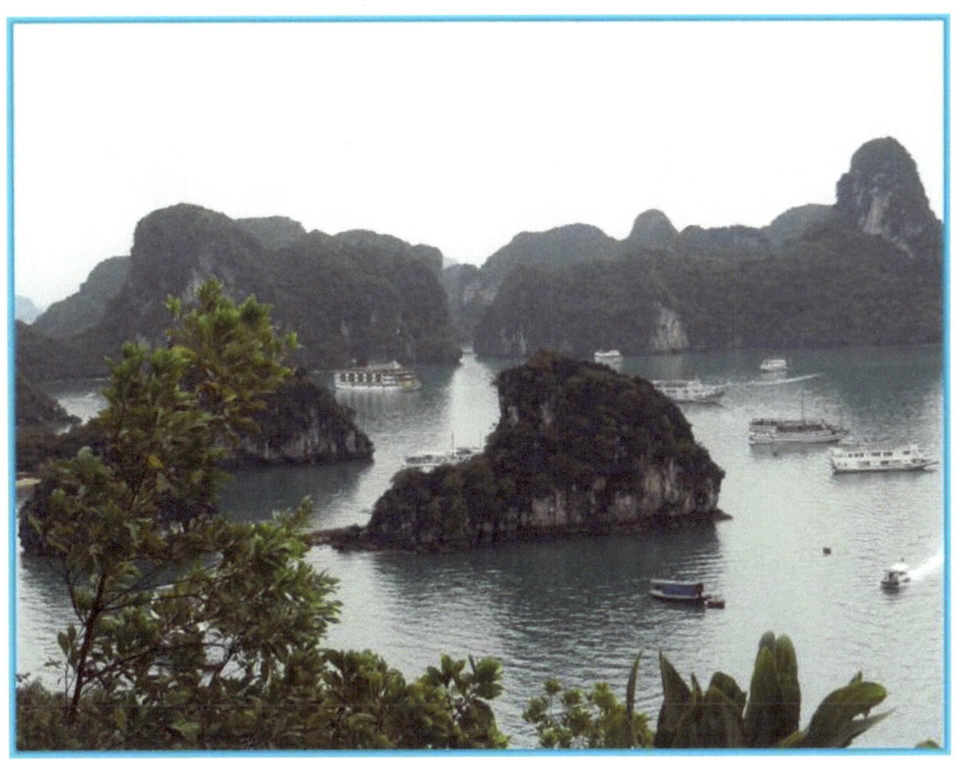

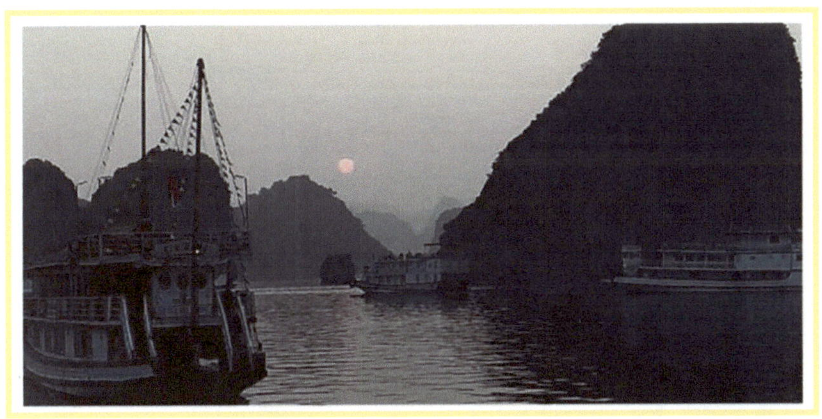

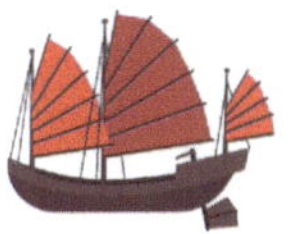

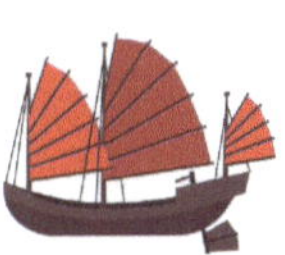

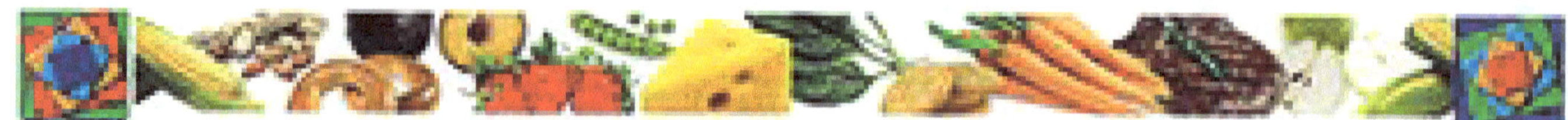

During the day, this young lady came alongside our boat to sell her wares. She had an array of soups, nuts, chips, and bananas, but one of her more popular items was her small selection of wines. You put her asking price in the net and she puts your sale back into it and hands it up to you. Quite a smart little business.

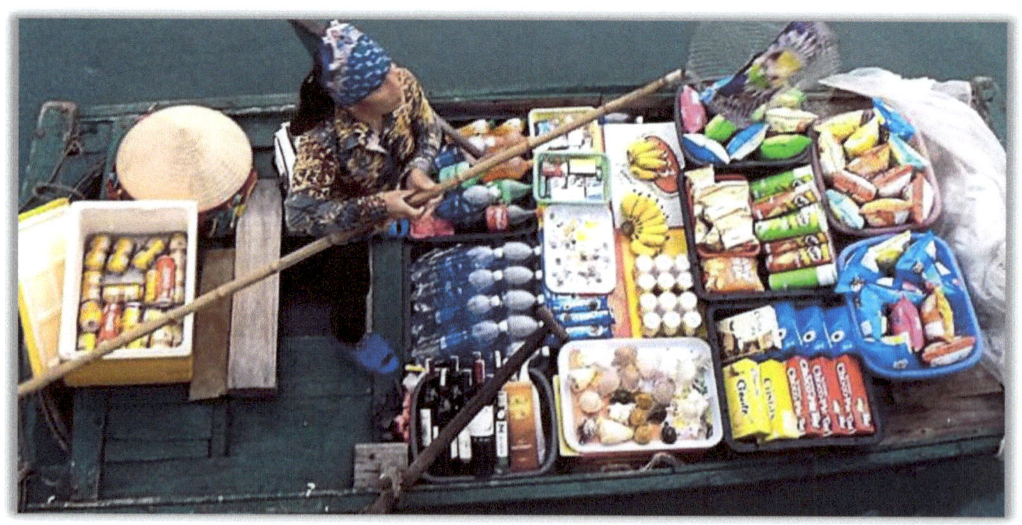

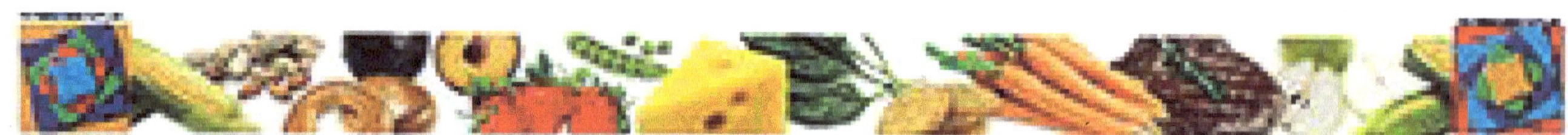

An overnight trip on Ha Long Bay provides a lot of interesting activities and demonstrations while shipboard. Our cook gave us a wonderful demonstration of the art of fruit and vegetable carving. As you can see, what he did to that carrot was beyond belief. He carved the round carrot and, after he had finished, he rolled it out into the shape of a net. Fruit and vegetable carvings are found at many upscale restaurants and resorts all over Vietnam.

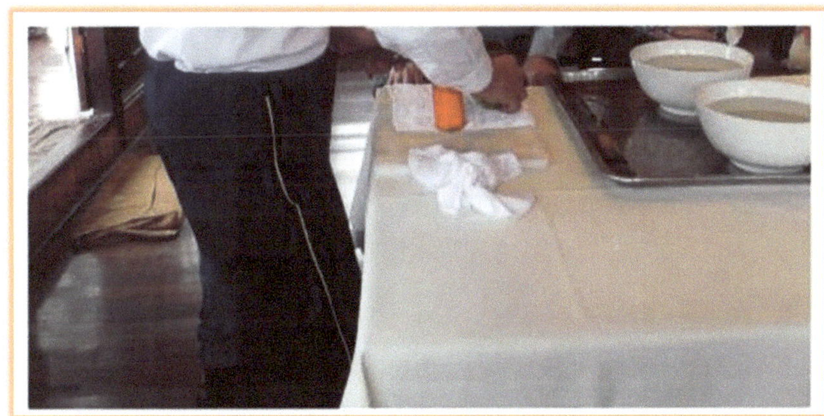

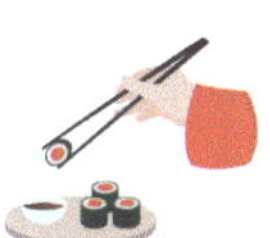

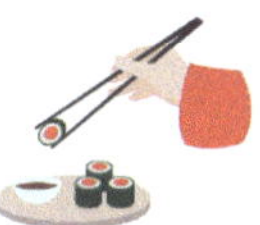

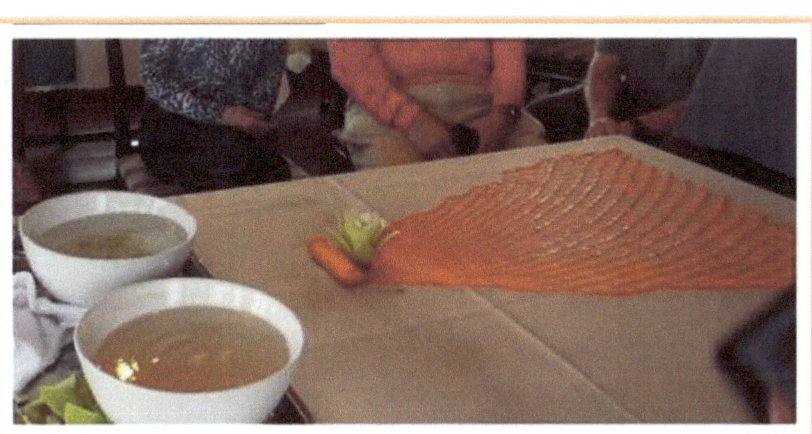

4—Hue

After our overnighter on Ha Long Bay, we went to the airport in Hanoi for our flight to Hue, which, for a little over 140 years, was the imperial capital of Vietnam. From 1802 until 1945, Hue served as the political capital of a unified Vietnam. It was also their center of culture and religion. Settlements in Hue date back over 1600 years. Much of what you will see are UNESCO World Heritage Sites. These countless historical sites and culturally important landmarks give every visitor ample opportunity to learn and capture riveting photographs. Much of Hue was destroyed in 1968 during the Tet Offensive, and thousands of its citizens were killed. But I must add, as an American visitor, it was a wonderful stop with beautiful pagodas and picturesque scenery, history, architecture, good food, and friendly people.

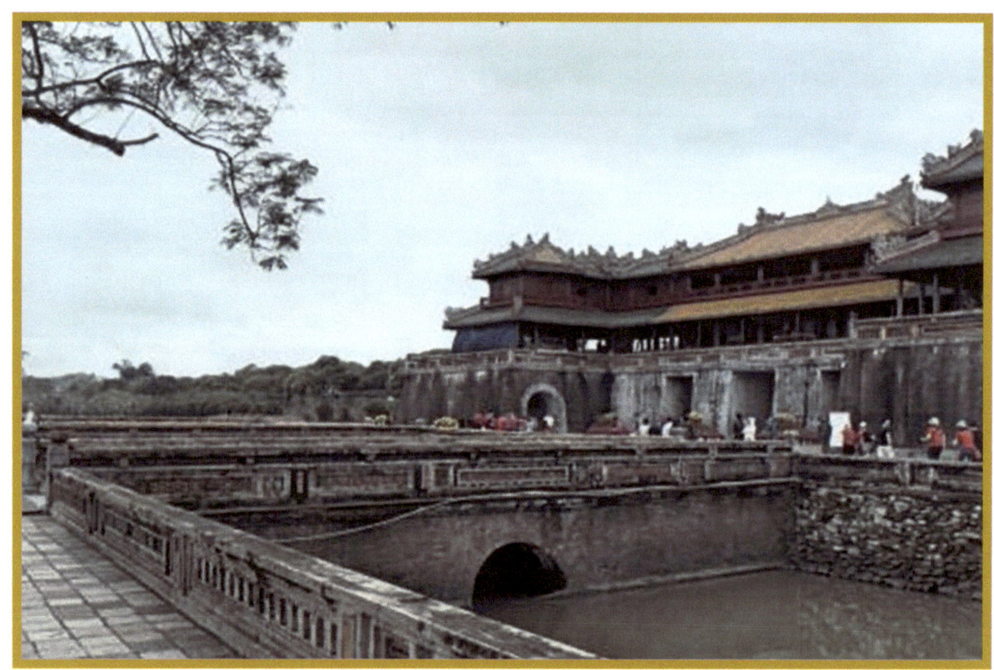

The Imperial City, as well as other sites in the older sections of Hue, are must-see places to go. You can still see sections of the moat surrounding the ancient walls of the citadel.

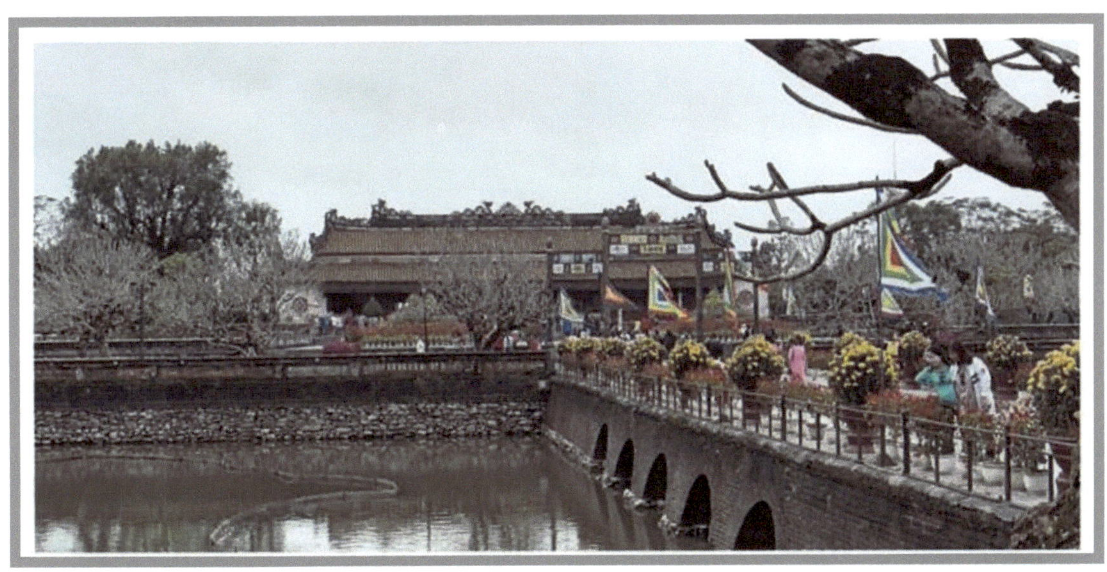

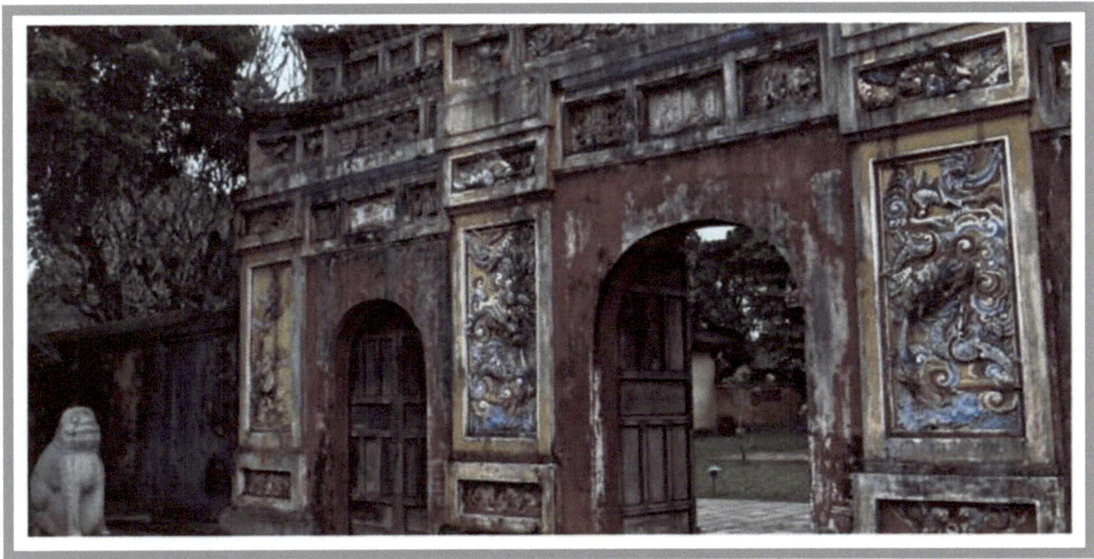

Past the ancient walls surrounding the Imperial City, or the citadel, of Hue, you can see the Forbidden Purple City, which was the emperor's home. There was so much to see while walking the grounds that I could not take it all in. One thing you should remember: do not forget to look up. While many others were photographing the ancient walls, flowers, and buildings, I looked up and captured the next picture. The designs and colors are amazing.

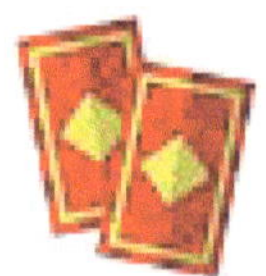
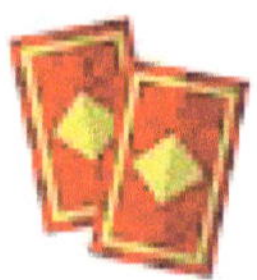
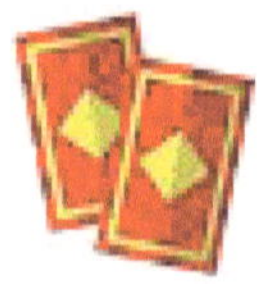
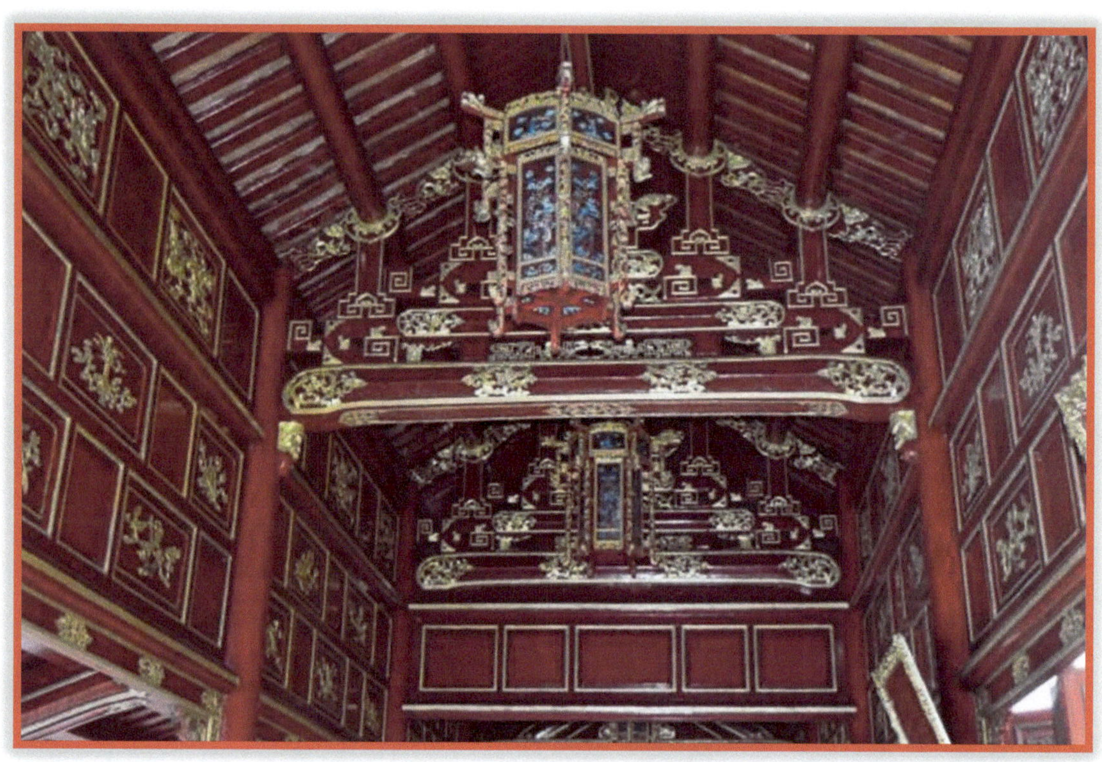
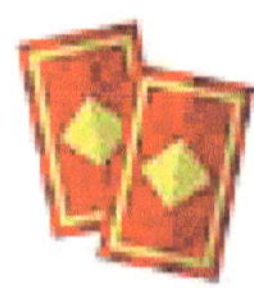
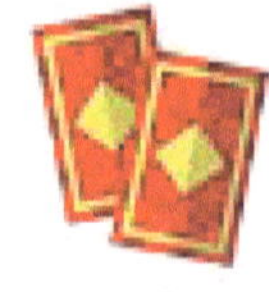

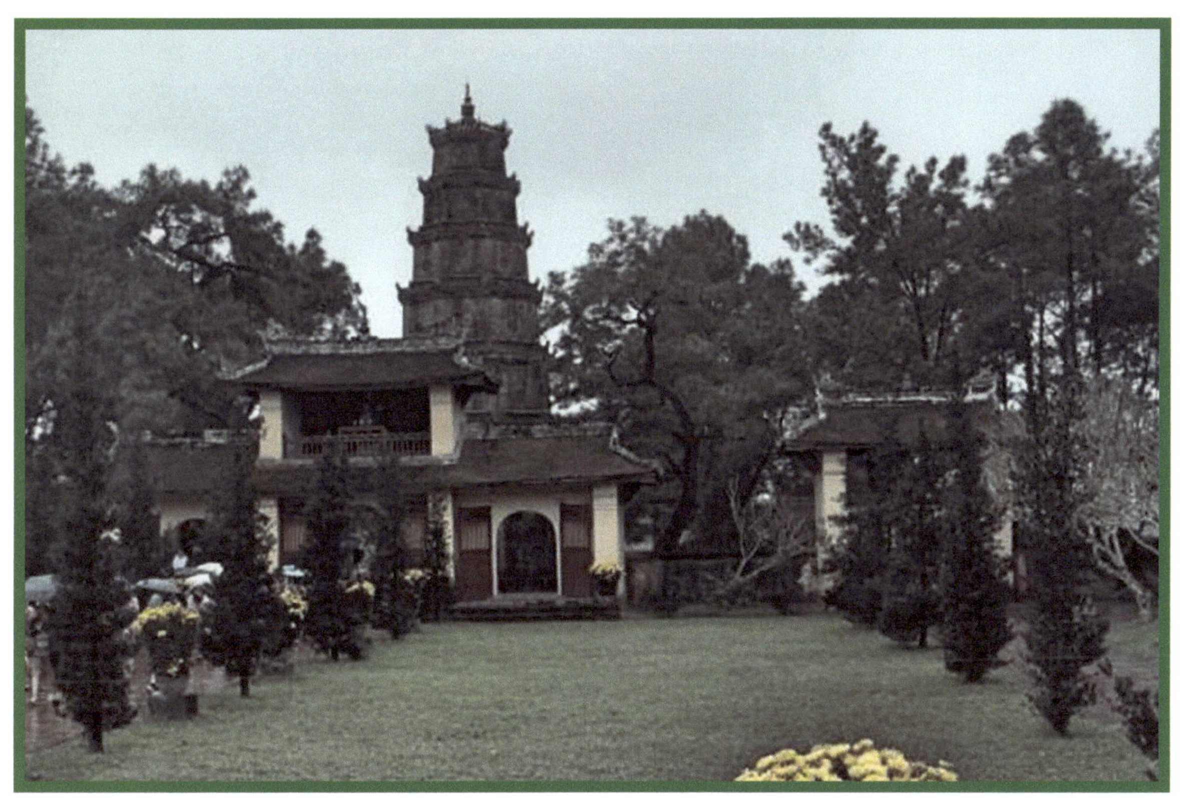

The seven-story Thien Mu Temple is one of the most photographed, historic temples in Vietnam and, as such, is the symbol of Hue. This is a good time to inform you about dress codes when entering or touring Buddhist temples such as this. Most temples and sacred places require most of the body to be covered. Tops must cover the shoulders and arms, and bottoms must reach the ankles. Most of the time, shoes are to be left outside. We were always warned ahead of time about the required dress. Several temples even had cloth robes available for everyone to put on over their shorts and tank tops. It is also a courtesy, sometimes a requirement, to take off your shoes when entering a private home.

Following are a few other photos of the scenic beauty in and around Hue for you to enjoy before we travel south to Hoi An.

This was one of my favorite scenes as we walked along the pathways located inside and outside the Citadel. The walks were always beautiful, and there were photographic opportunities everywhere you looked.

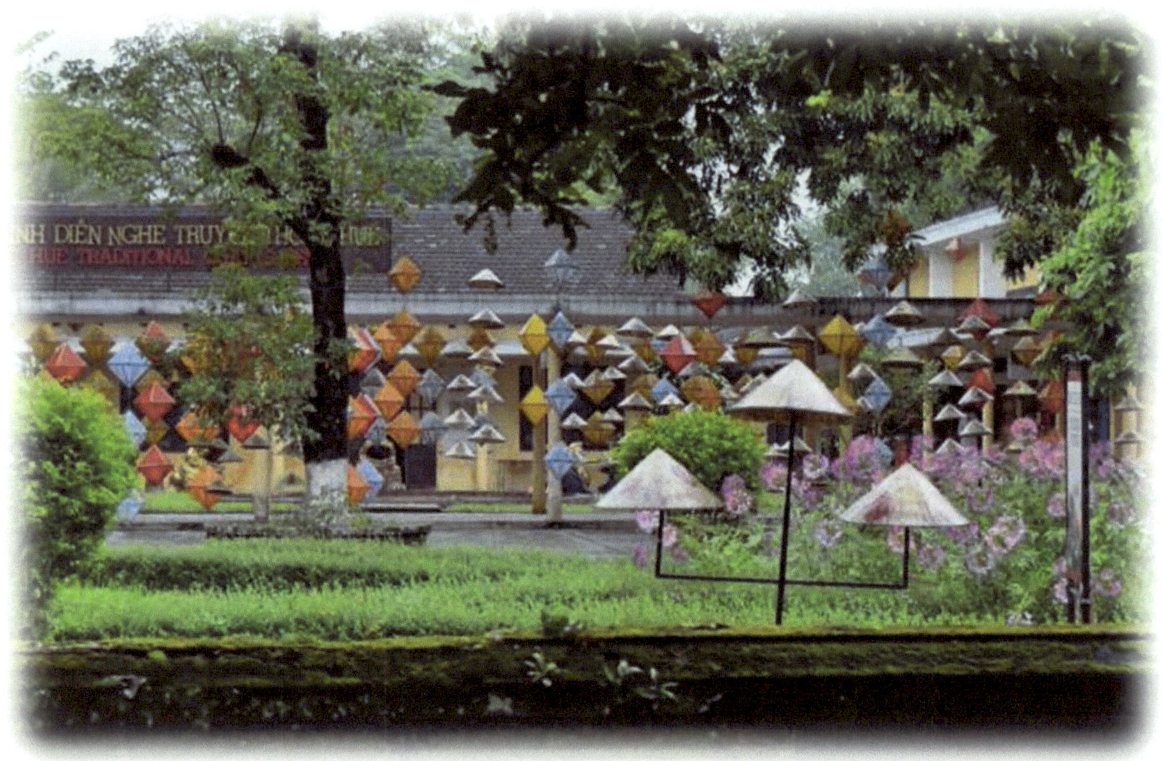

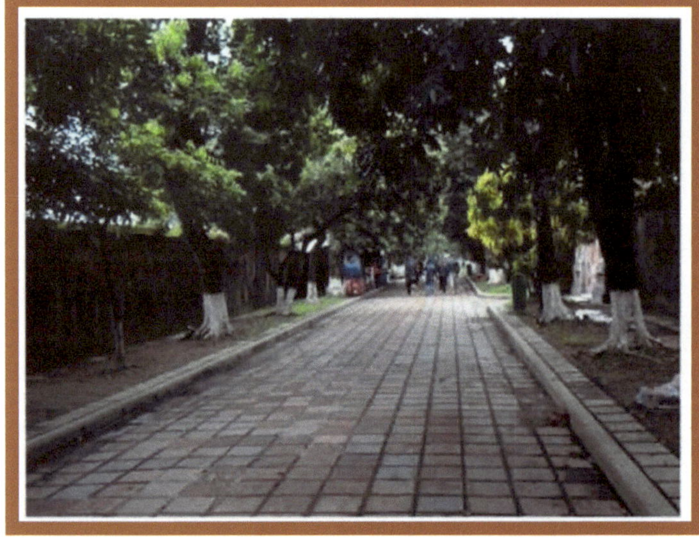

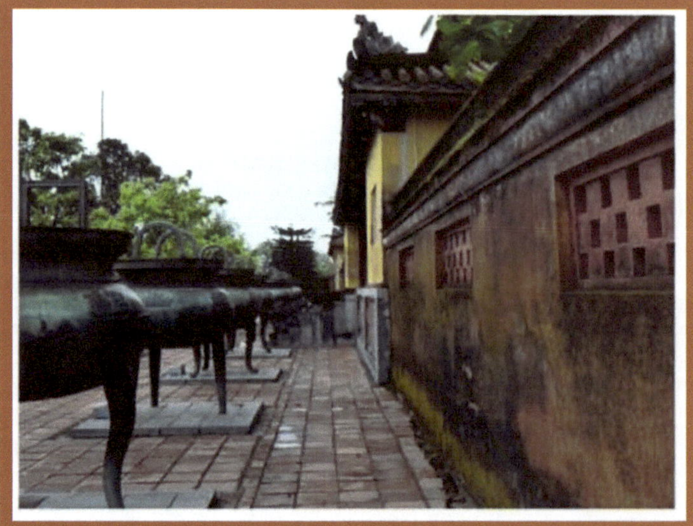

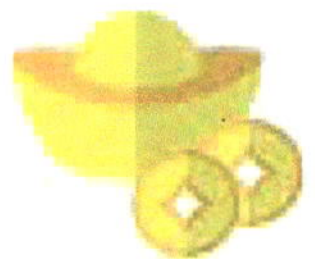
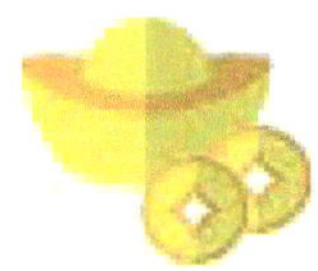
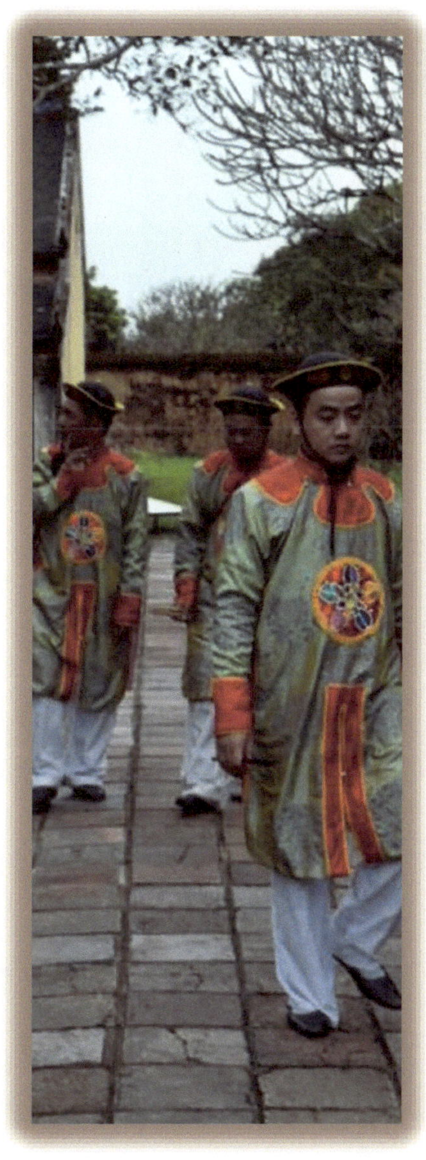
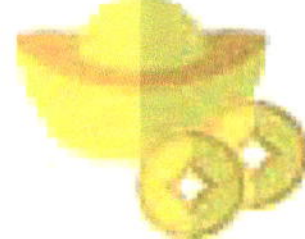
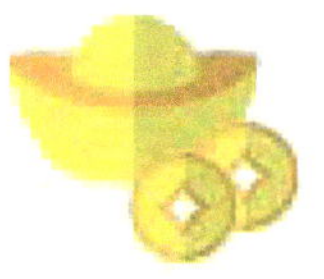

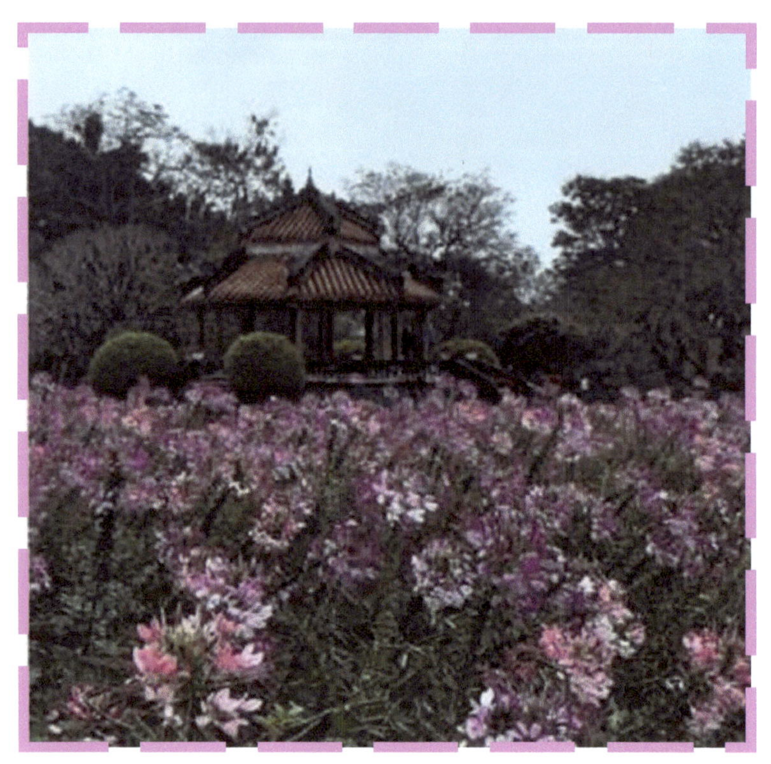

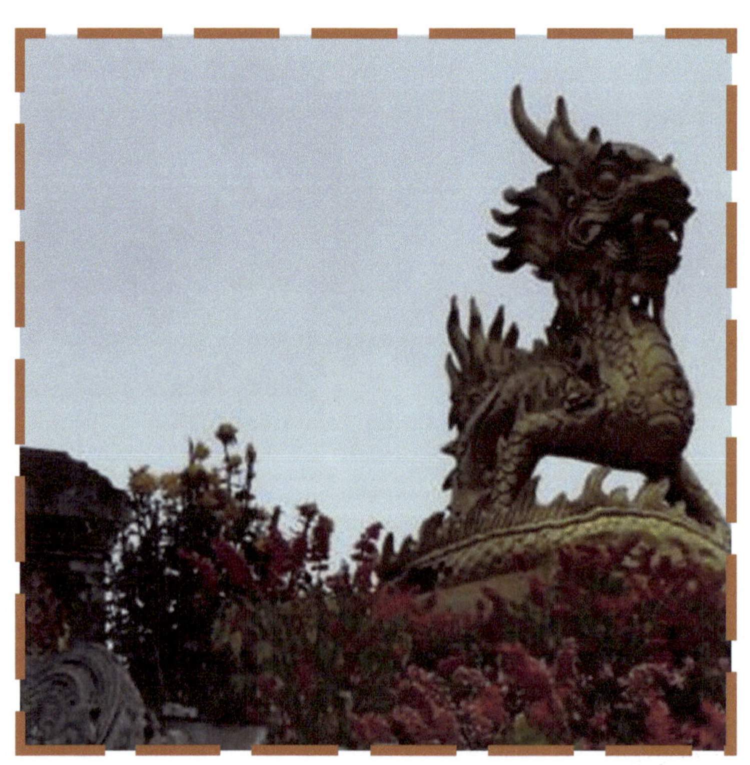

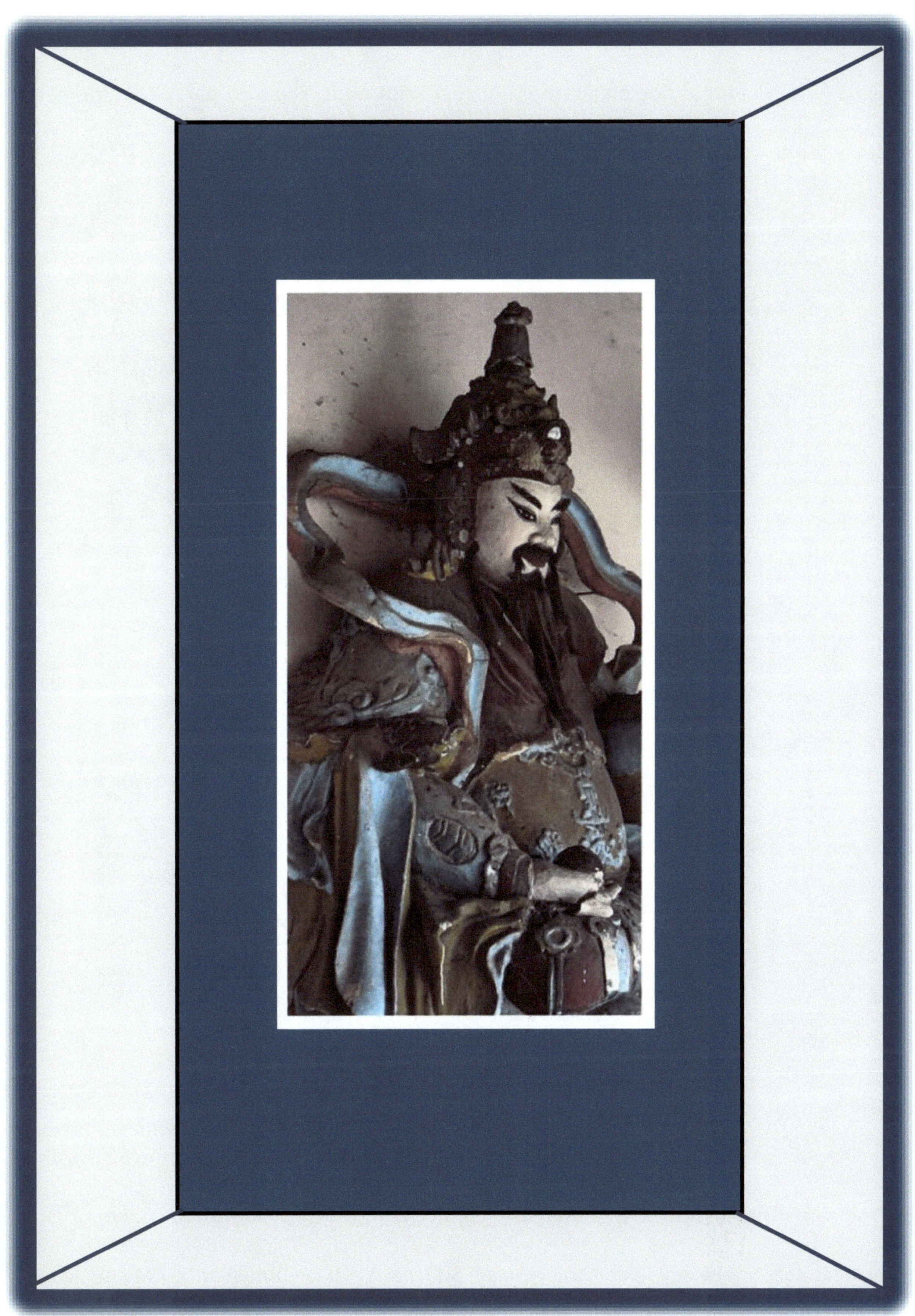

During my travels, I love to go out on any river that happens to be nearby. The Perfume River, or Song Huon in Vietnamese, flowing right through the middle of Hue was no exception. We had a great riverboat ride on a rather unusual watercraft. The best part of exploring the rivers, of course, is seeing local life on the water up close and personal.

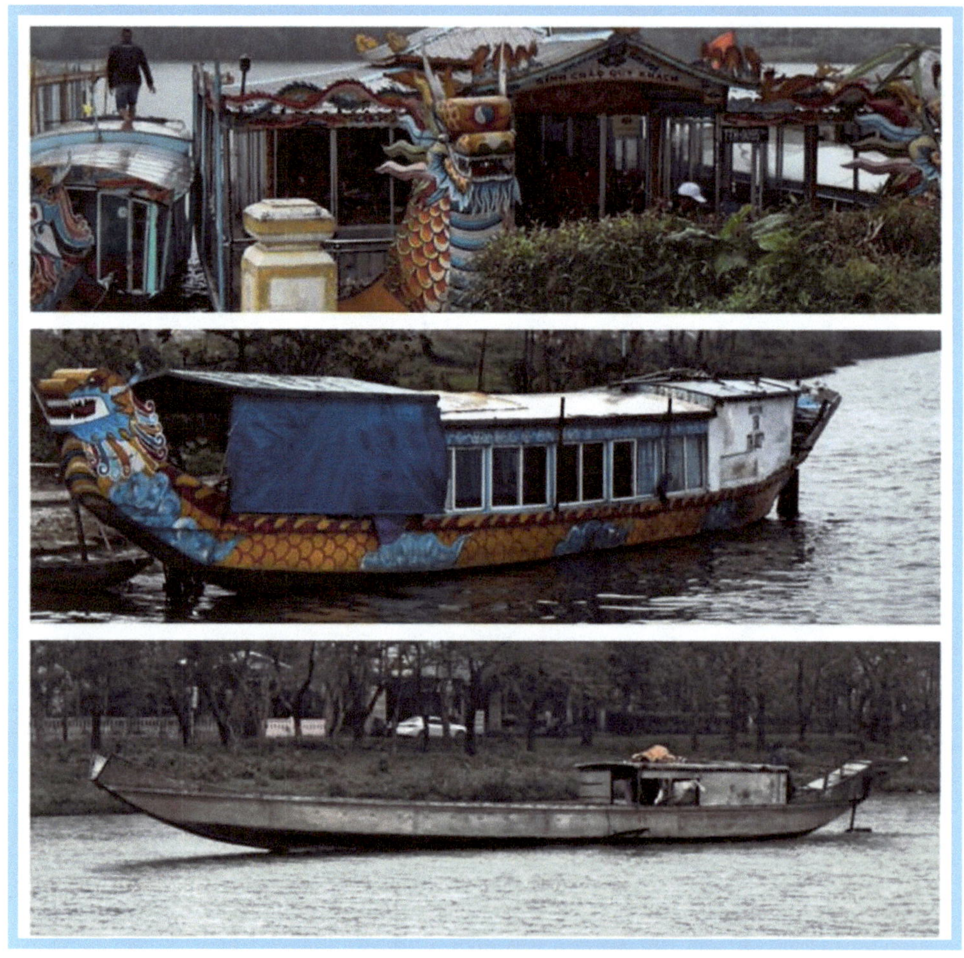

One of the advantages of being part of a small group tour is discovering places like this. You might never stop at this unassuming, out-of-the-way store on your own. It is a small, local store that sells everything from SIM cards to an unusual variety of local, alcoholic beverages, one, of which, no one cared to try.

In Vietnam, poisonous snake liquor is one of those traditional drinks the Vietnamese believe have medicinal qualities. Many believe this drink can cure everything from bad eyesight to baldness. The alcohol varies from hard liquor, close to ethanol, to rice wine. Do you have backaches? Digestive issues? Problems with fertility? Many believe this is just what you need! I think I'll pass on this one. We all did!!

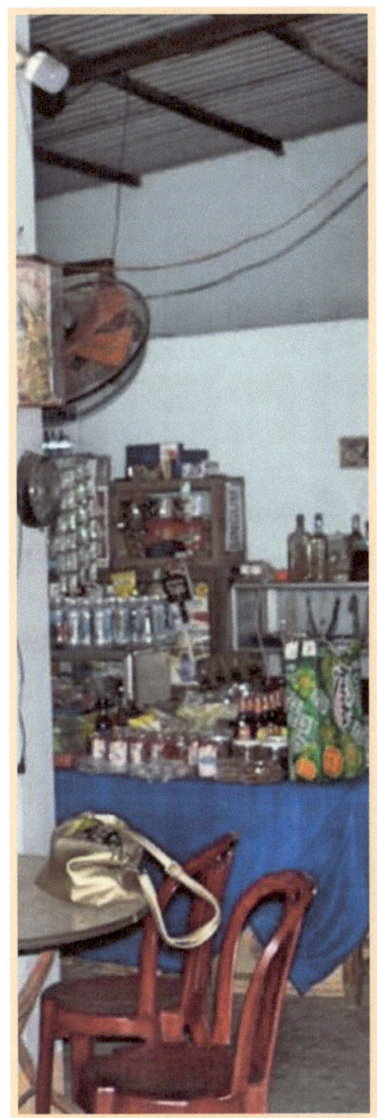

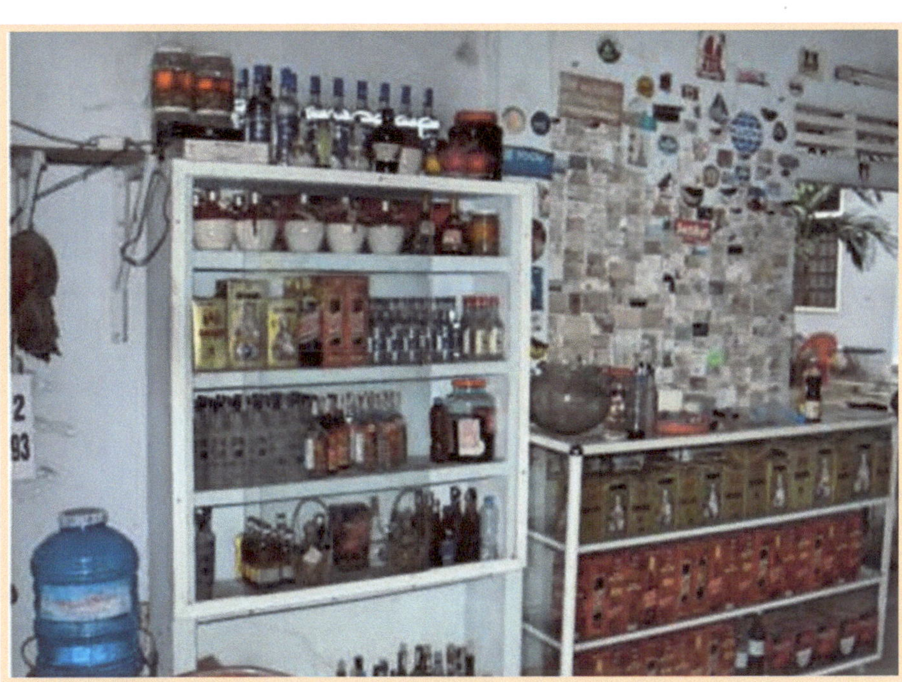

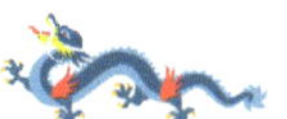

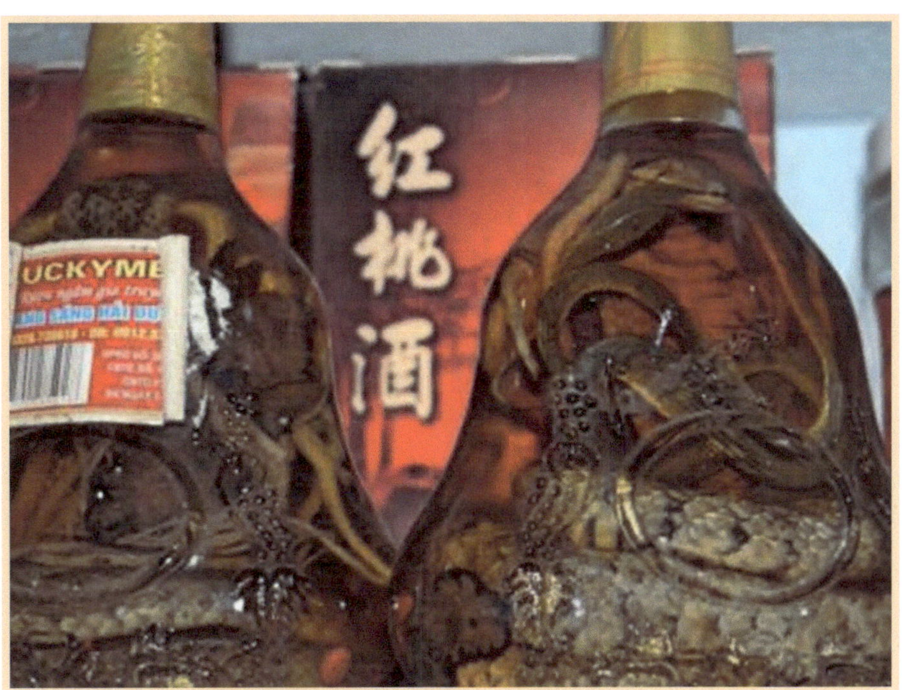

5—Hoi An

After we visited Hue, we drove toward Hoi An next, stopping at China Beach and then Danang. China Beach was the fictional, critically acclaimed, TV medical drama set during the war. The actual beach is in the city of Da Nang, and its local name is My Khe. China Beach was the nickname given by American soldiers. Unfortunately, the TV show was canceled after four years due to low audience ratings. Many thought it was ahead of its time.

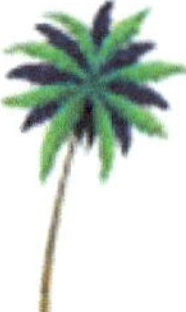

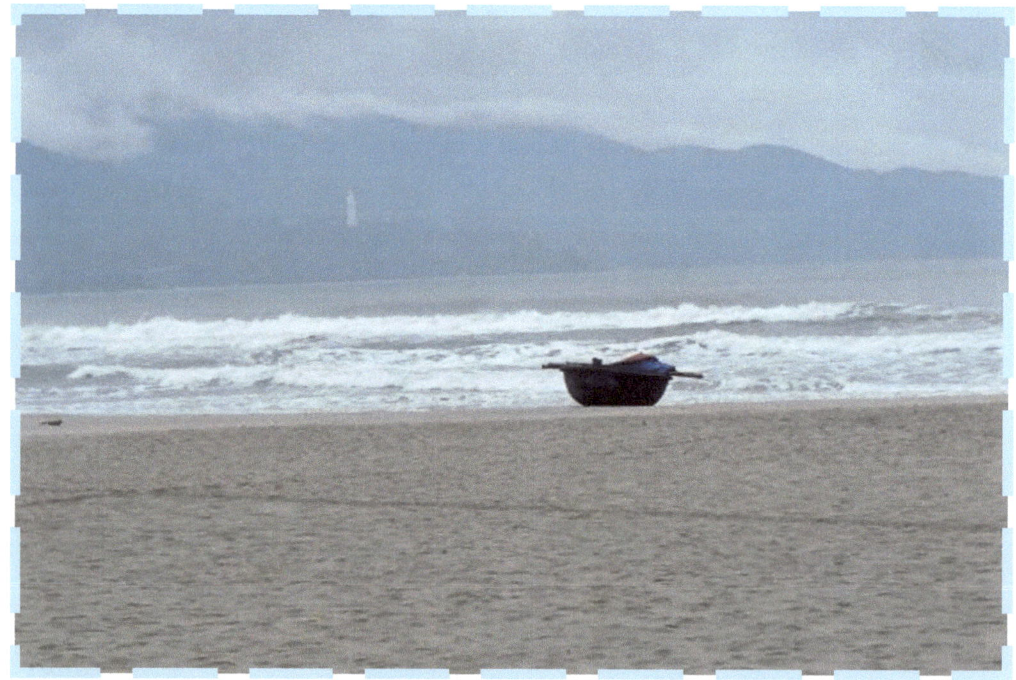

I am not sure what I expected to see at China Beach or, for that matter, in and around Danang, Nha Trang, and Cam Ranh Bay in general. It should have come as no surprise to see the expansive development of condos, golf courses, hotels, and more. What I had known as a war zone is now a tourist mecca. In some of these areas, there are signs in Russian, as this is a popular spot for their winter visits. These areas are also popular with Chinese tourists. The displays and menu signs at restaurants are all in Russian, Chinese, and English because, after all, we are all just tourists, no matter where we venture from.

Hoi An is still one of my favorite places in all of Asia. From their restaurants, to the beautiful areas of Old Town Hoi An, to the scenery on and along the Thu Bon River, it is magical. I remember this particular restaurant, not only for its food but also for its colorful décor.

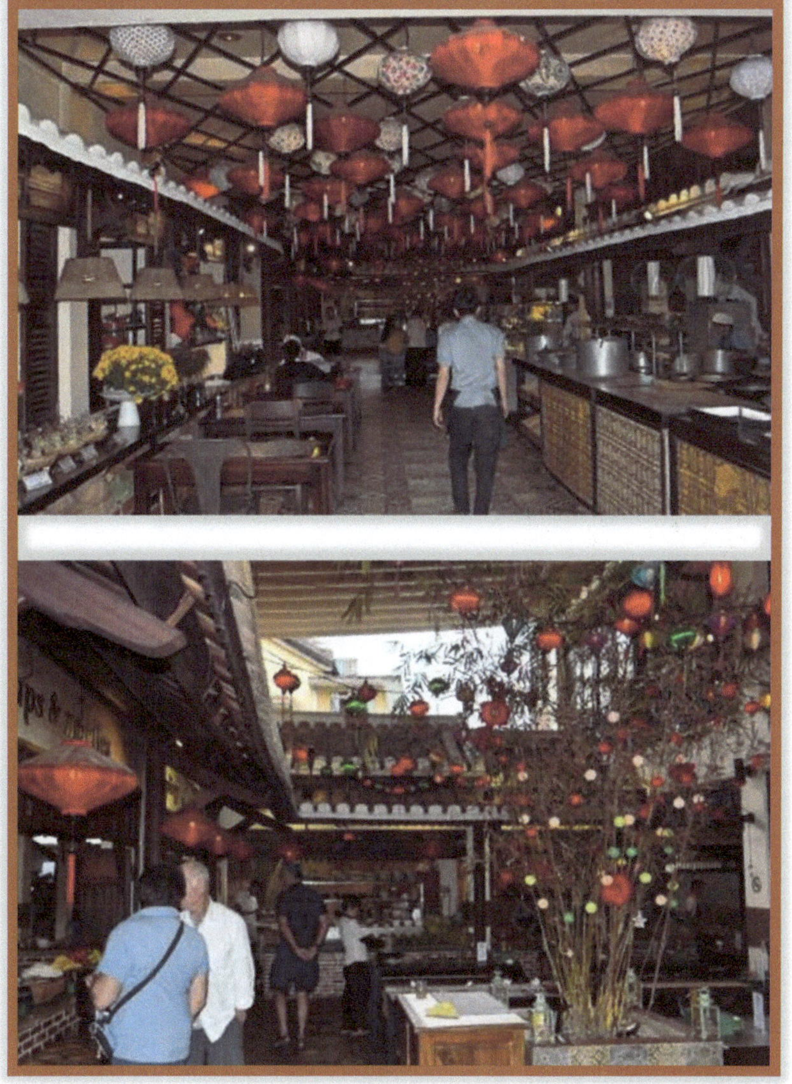

One of the most enjoyable walks during my two-week tour was when I walked along the narrow streets and alleys of Hoi An's Old Town. During our walk, our guide told us a little about the history of Hoi An, telling of the historic houses and buildings that have been maintained as close to the originals as possible. These historic areas were influenced by traders and merchants from Persia, Arabia, India, Japan, and China. Later, Christian missionaries also influenced the architectural designs.

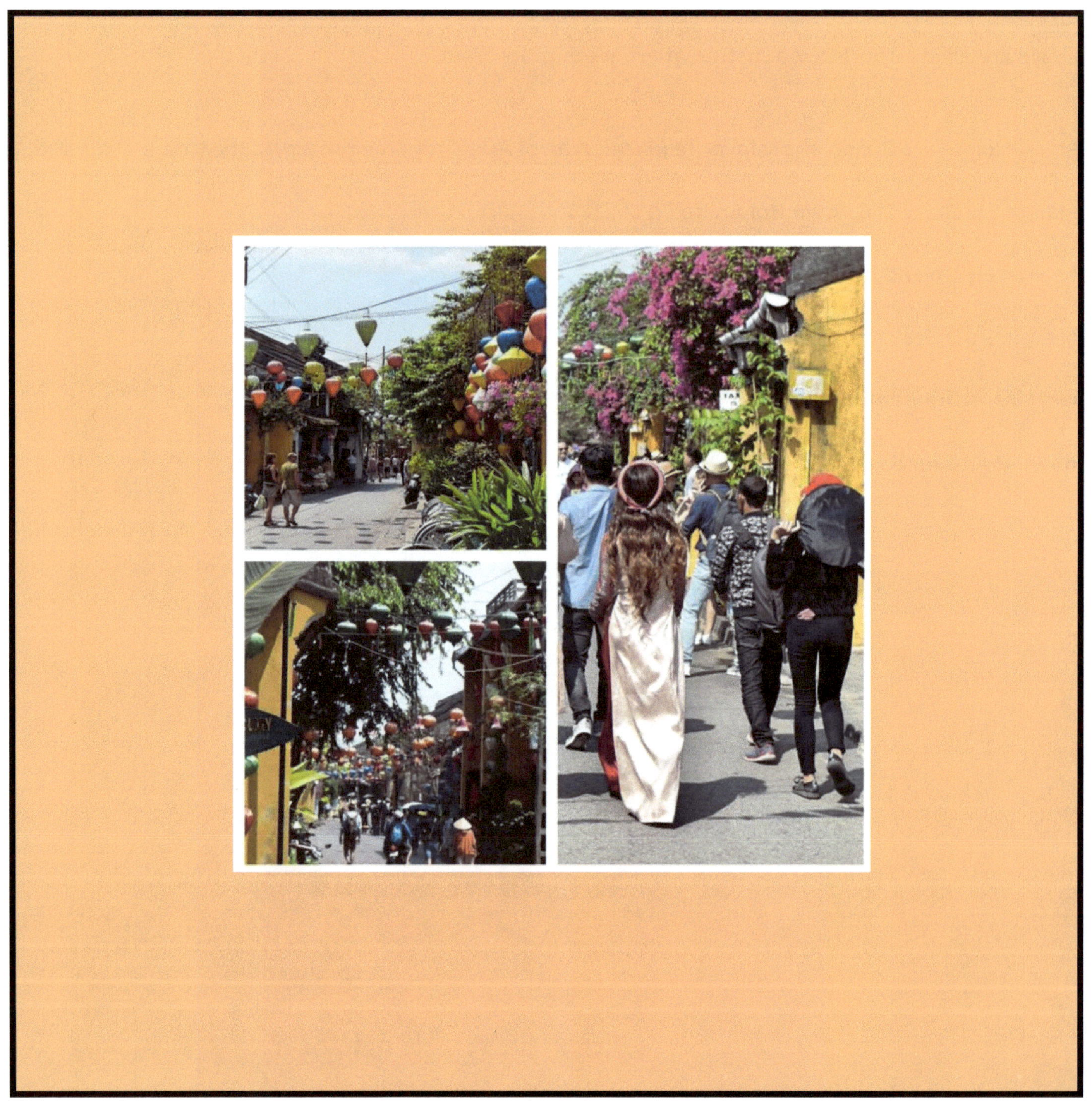

We were told that, as modern as Vietnam has become—perhaps *too* Westernized—Vietnamese women are generally still modest and may not appreciate having their photos taken without their permission, even more so with older adults and men. For young women, this part of Confucian values is an important part of their traditional upbringing. Imagine our surprise when we were allowed to photograph these young people.

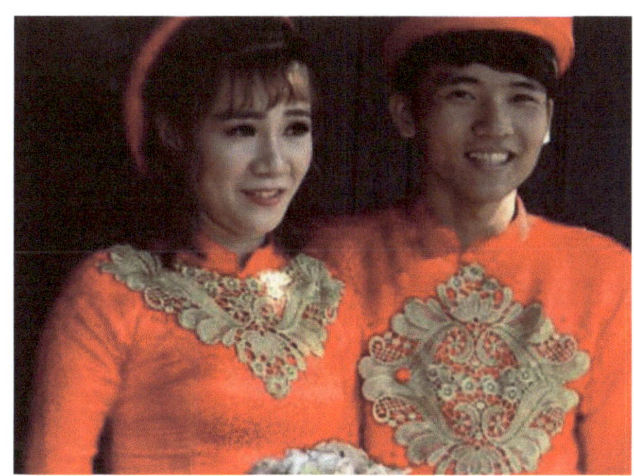

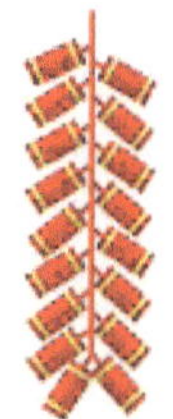

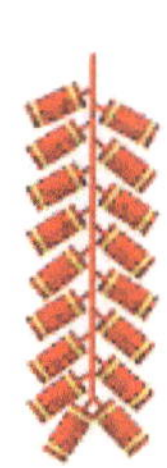

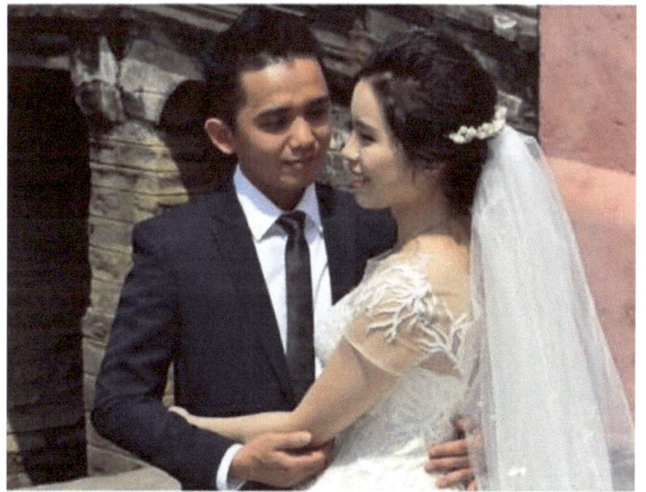

The young couple with a new bride in white graciously allowed our group to photograph them, alongside their wedding photographer, as they posed in Hoi An's old town. It was a real joy watching the two of them interact with our group and, when we were finished, our tour guide took a group photo of all of us with the bride and groom in the middle. We were rather shocked! The other young couple was nearby and wore beautiful outfits which we had seen several times. All over the UNESCO Hoi An Old Village, young couples wore traditional, colorful outfits they had rented for their photographs.

These six young girls were sitting near one of the more picturesque, historic buildings and having their pictures taken by friends or family.

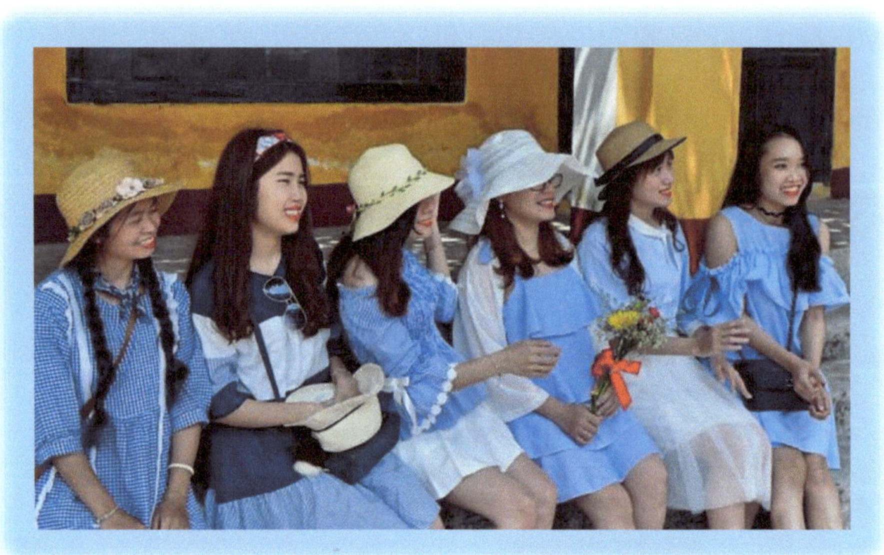

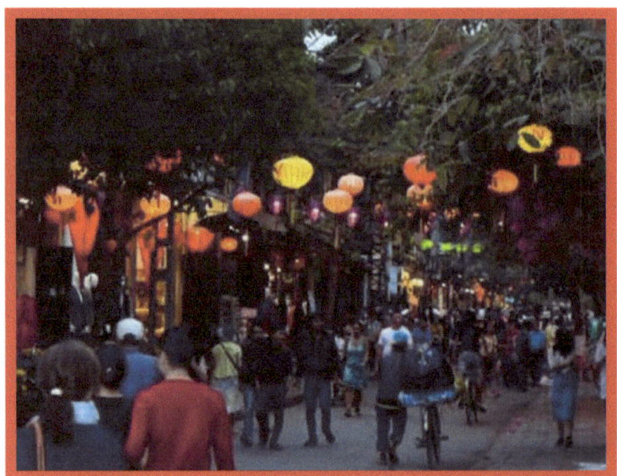

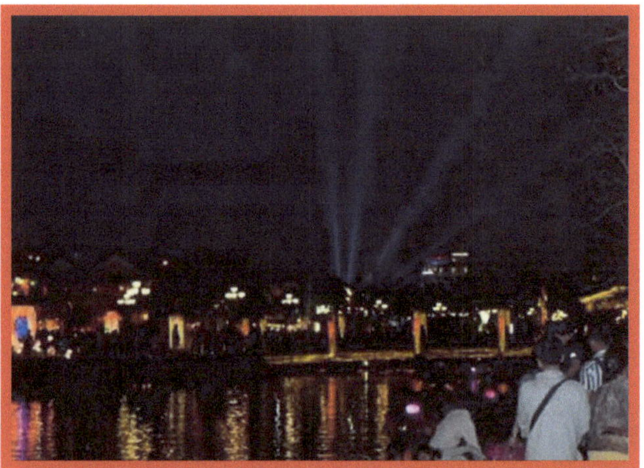

After embarking upon long walks, eating great food, and learning more than you could ever think possible, make sure you save plenty of energy to go out, either with your tour or on your own, at dusk or nighttime. Everything changes, and the scenery is spectacular. The photos directly above and the one on the next page were taken along the Thu Bon River as well as in Old Town Hoi An.

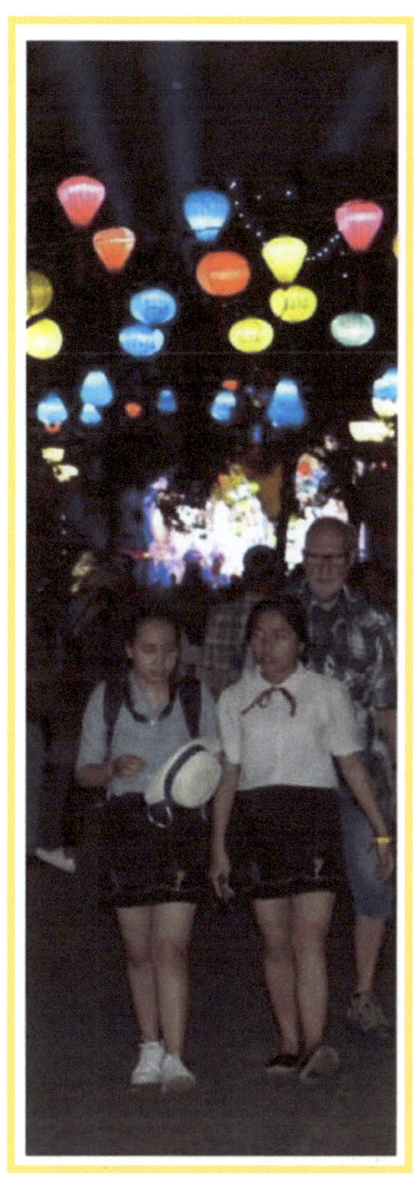

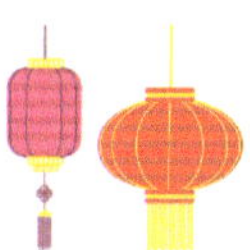

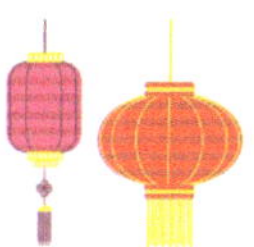

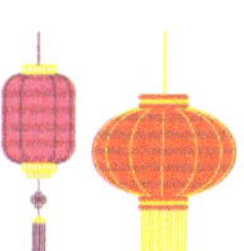

If your tour includes a boat ride, or if you have time on your own, you will get to experience another fun river. If traveling alone, there are opportunities for boat rides along every riverfront. The Thu Bon River is popular with visitors and locals alike. There are historic, local villages along the shore, a wide variety of markets everywhere, and boats of every type out on the water, either at work or travel.

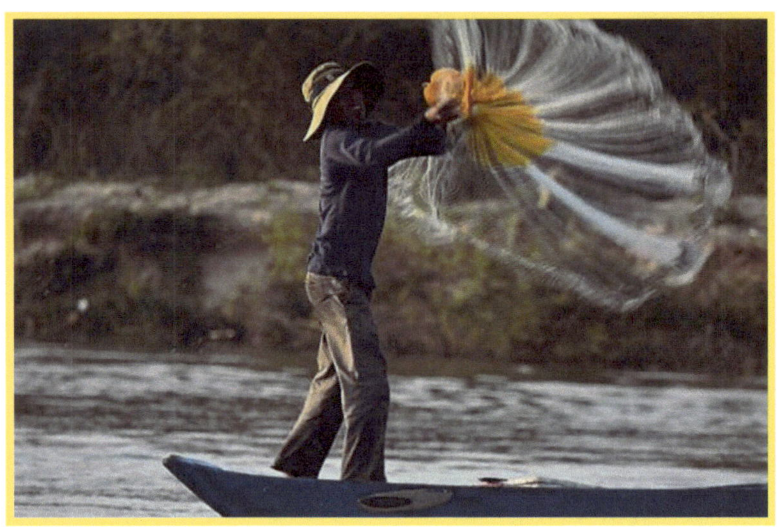

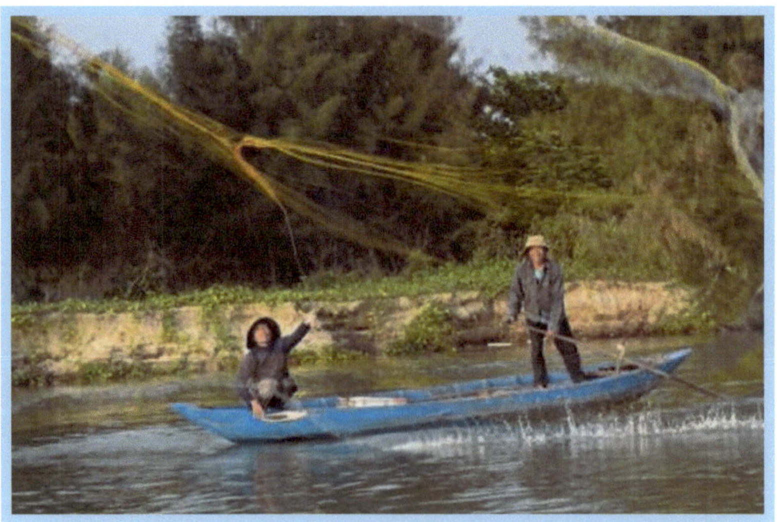

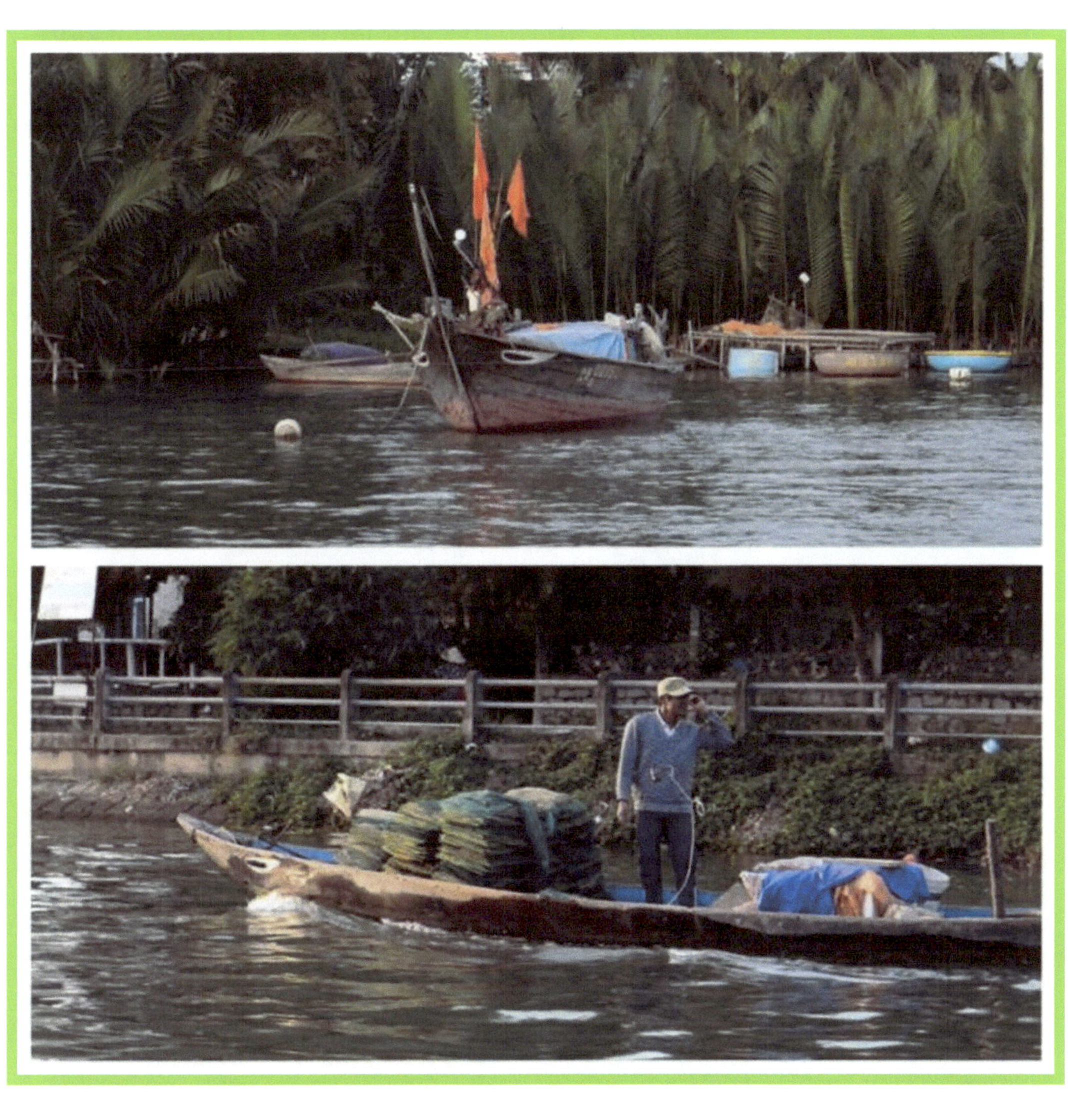

6—Getting to the Markets

There is no shortage of markets in Vietnam. While some are wet markets, many offer an unending supply of dry goods such as noodles, spices, different types of rice, and even fruits and vegetables. Most of the smaller markets I encountered were family-run operations where the whole family could be found working. The method by which the Vietnamese people transport their products to market is interesting in and of itself. This young lady was carrying a full load of oranges.

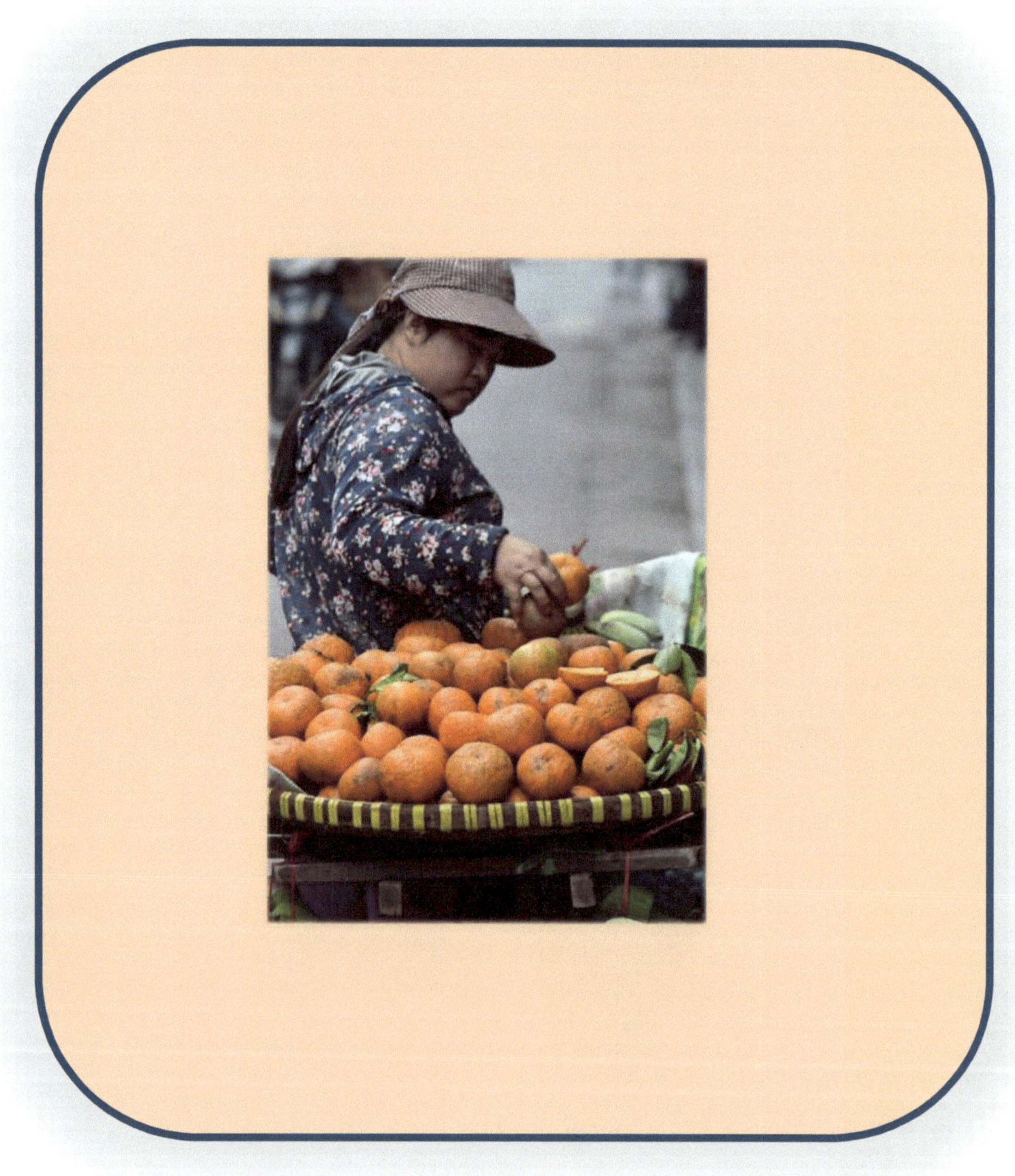

This guy just happened to be passing our bus when I saw him out the window. He looked quite at ease with a full load of uncaged ducks heading off to the market. I still marvel at the way the ducks stayed put as he zipped by us.

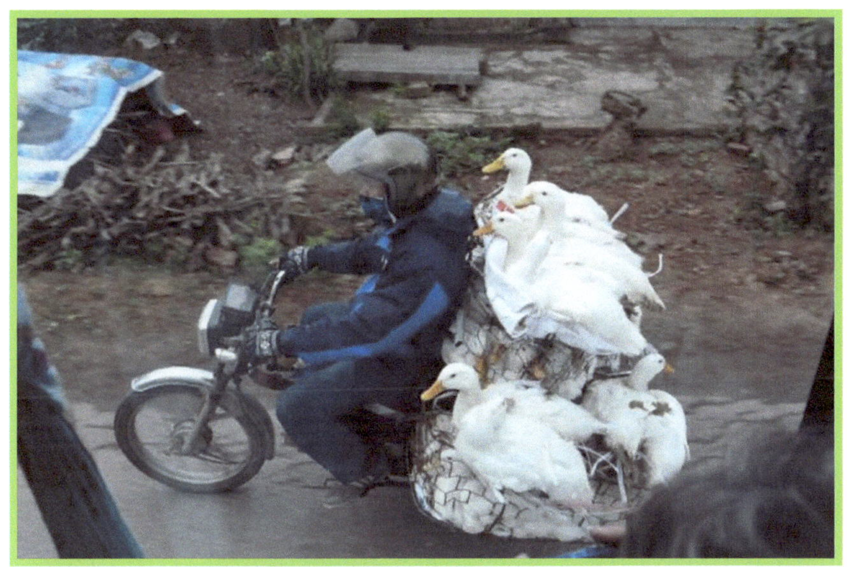

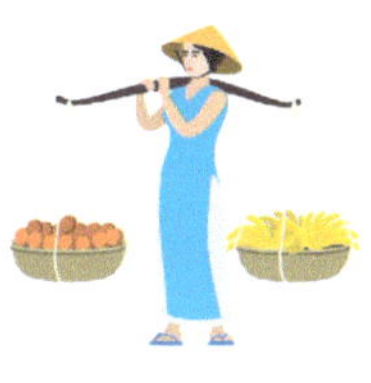

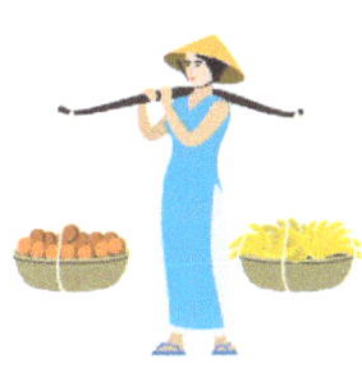

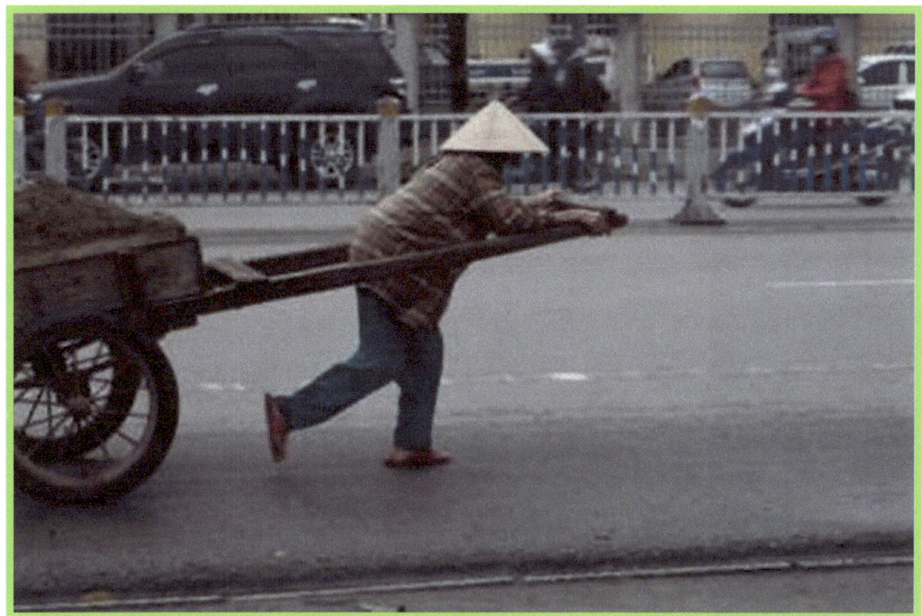

The picture of the woman pulling the cart full of sand is typical of what can be seen anywhere in Vietnam, regardless if you are in a large city or a small village. I think the reason I like this photo is because of the contrast you can see from the top of the photo to her on the bottom. New and old, what one cannot afford versus what one can. And then we have bicycles, which can be seen carrying sacks of rice, and other items, stacked so high as to pass the rider's head.

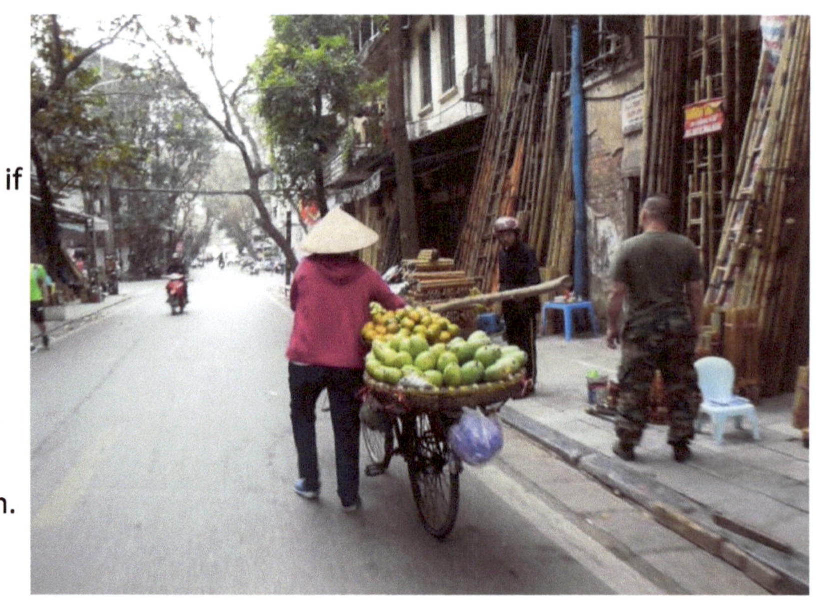

What a sight to see—all the various modes of transportation carrying foodstuffs to both small and large markets alike! I loved wandering through the aisles of the many markets, both inside and out. You can buy anything from durian to dried crickets or from worms to water-melons. Wet markets sold every kind of meat imaginable—some of which you, perhaps, may not want to imagine.

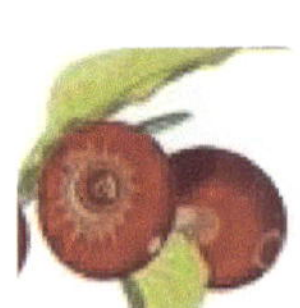

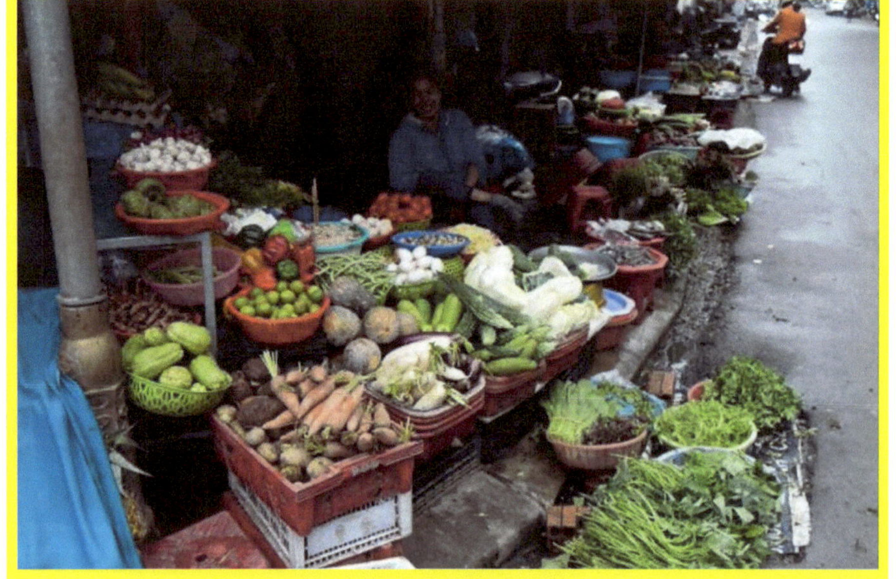

Vegetable stands, such as these, can be found on almost every street corner. You can also find stands like this one, situated beneath many sunshades.

Many of the indoor markets are like big warehouses under a tin roof and have all the things required for cooking over long periods. One can also find a wide variety of work and leisure clothing in these markets. There are umbrellas, wallets, purses, hats, and coats right next to dried worms and bugs, fish, meat, rice, and everything in between.

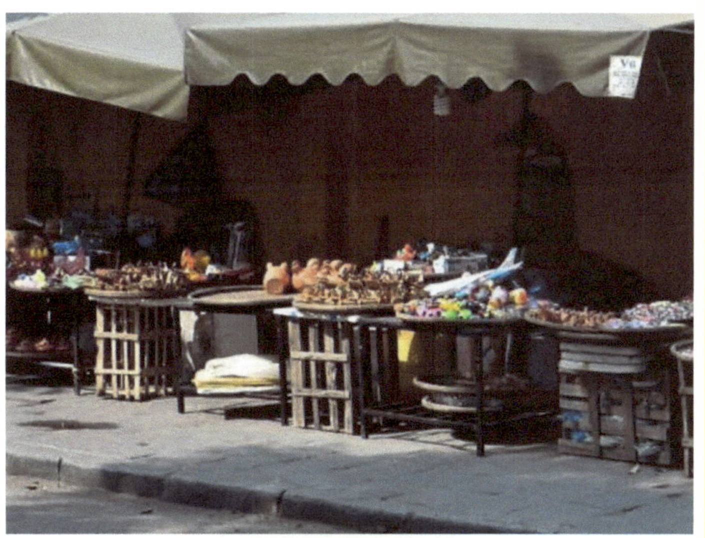

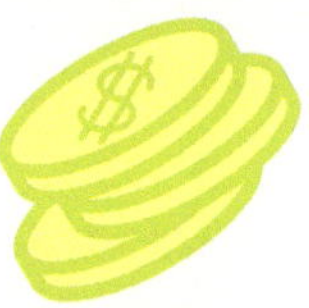

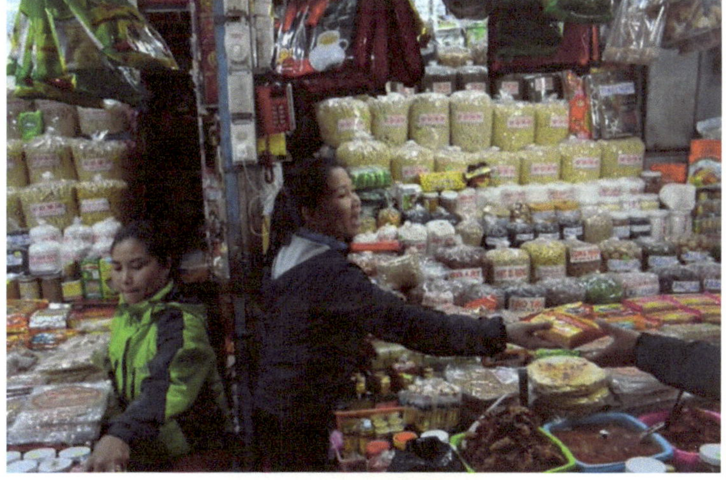

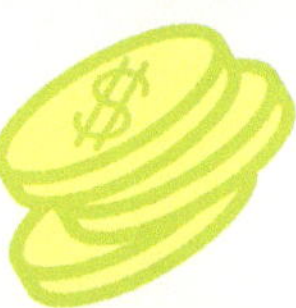

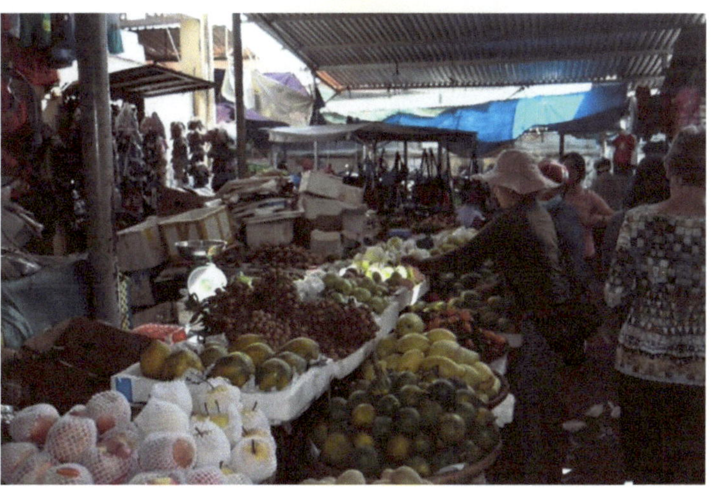

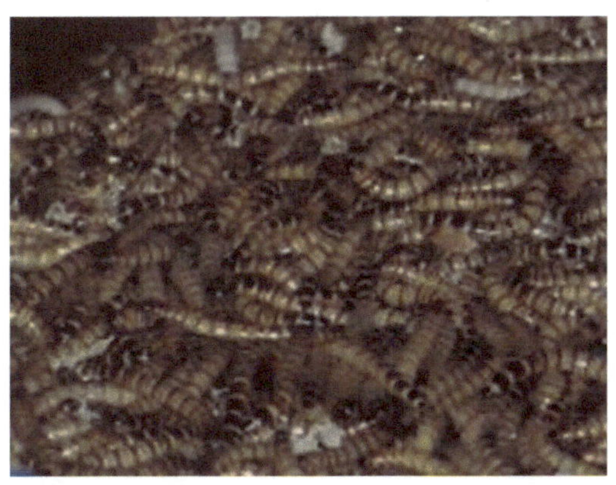

Not my cup of tea—I'll pass on these! Although I did try some of the spicy, dried crickets that are sold in small bags, like our potato chips. They were quite good!

7—Silk

Near Hoi An, we had an opportunity to see how silk is produced. While there, we were also able to observe some of the historic equipment used to capture and weave the silk into colorful cloth. Hoi An Silk Village is another must-see, especially if you venture out on your own and are in search of the next attraction. The Silk Village is said to be the oldest village of its kind, over 300 years old. In the village, you can follow the entire process of silk making as the silk takes its journey from the mulberry tree to a silk scarf. You can also learn historical information about the ways of the Champa people. Next, we will visit My Son to learn about Cham. This living museum is less than two miles from Old Town Hoi An.

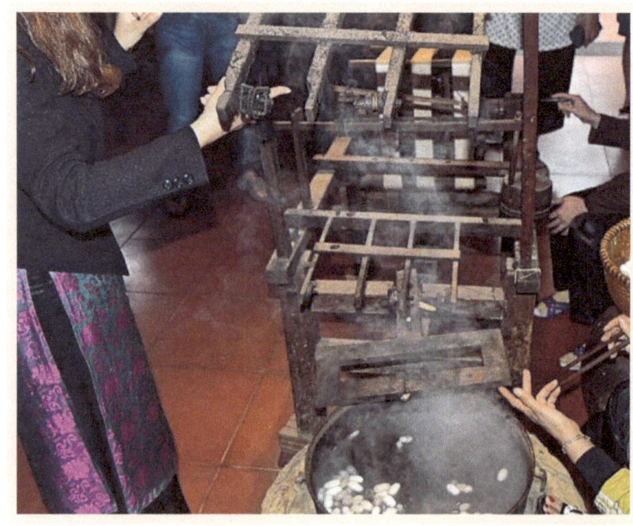

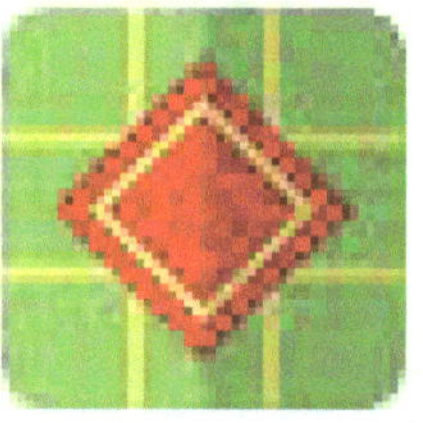

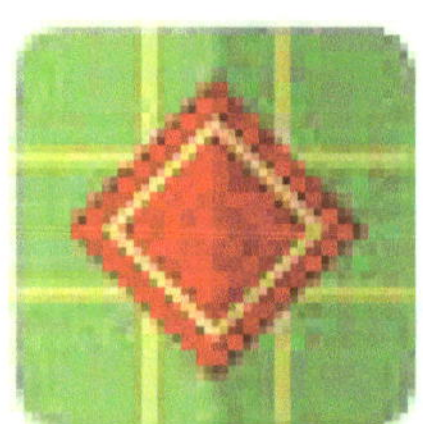

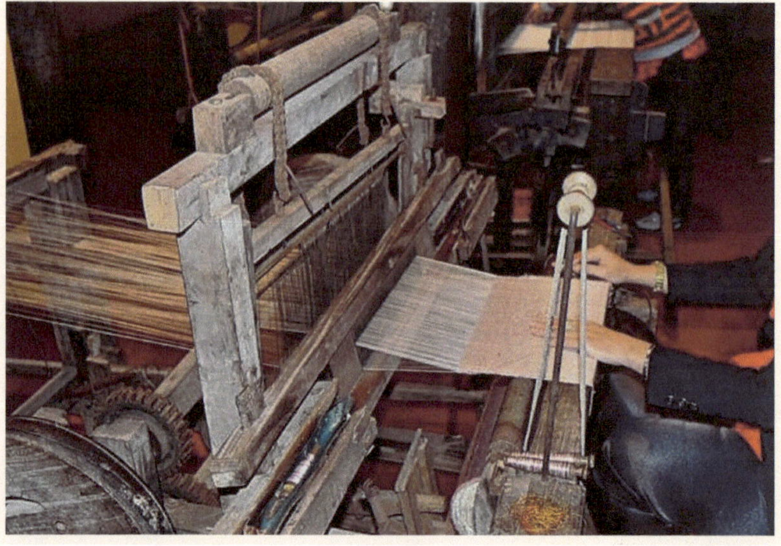

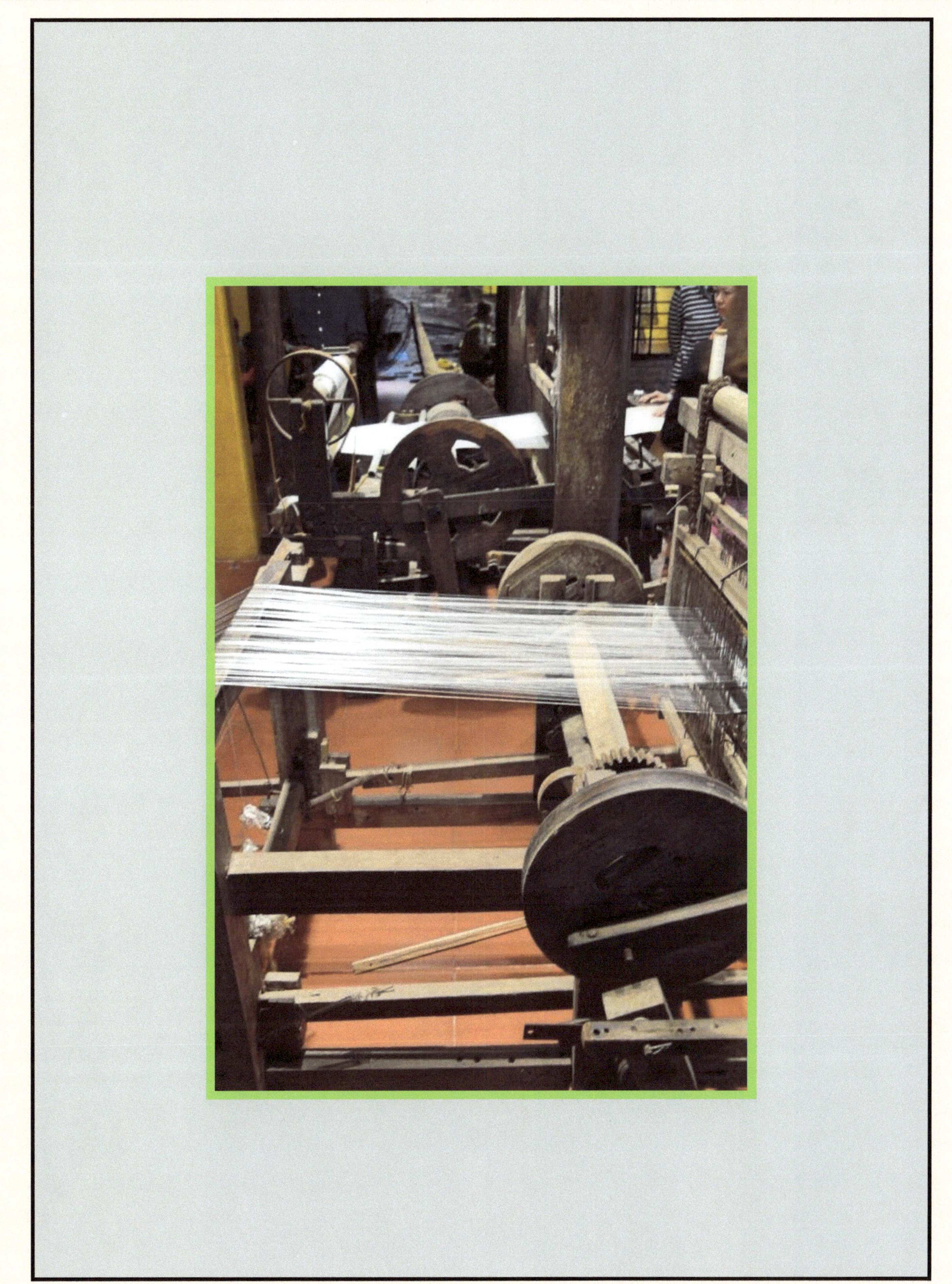

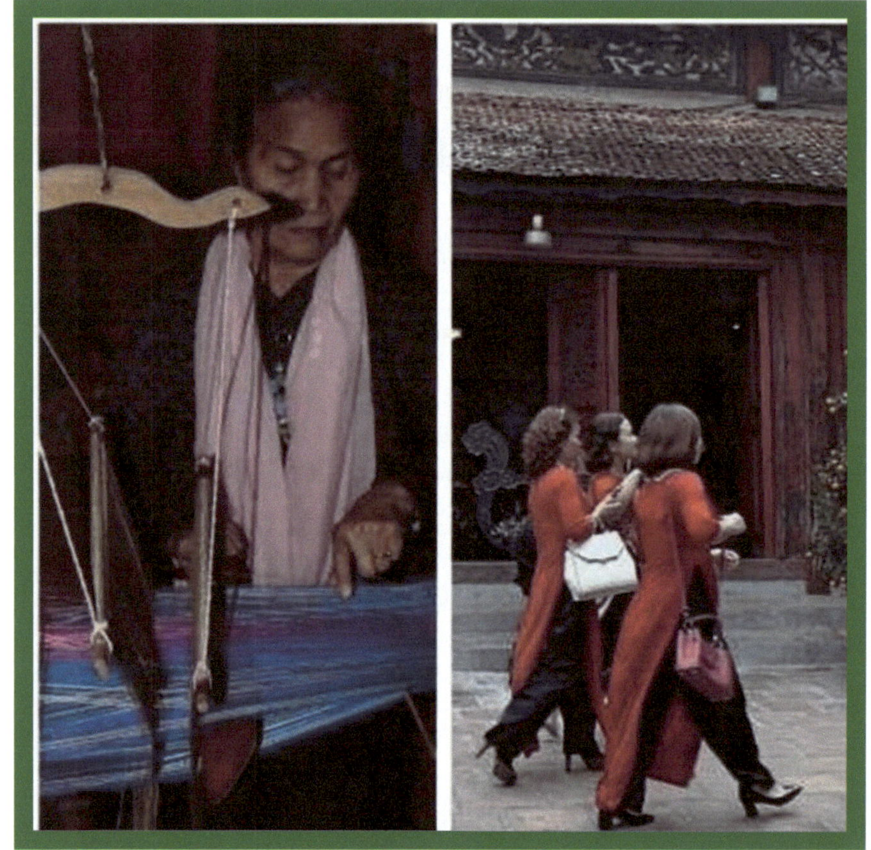

8—My Son Sanctuary

One of the most unique places to see in Vietnam is the Champa Kingdom Ruins located in the My Son Sanctuary. It is a UNESCO Cultural Heritage site that dates from the 4th to the 13th centuries and holds around 70 towers, temples, and other types of ruins. This area is also the source of the Thu Bon River that flows through Hoi An. These ruins were first discovered by French archaeologists. After the reunification of Vietnam, there was an increase in conservation efforts, since the entire area is subject to flooding and other weather extremes.

Other issues that impede conservation efforts are the numerous discoveries of unexploded ordnance from the war. For this reason, there are warning signs that tell people to stay on the developed trails. This entire site reminded me of Siem Reap, located in Cambodia, but on a much smaller scale.

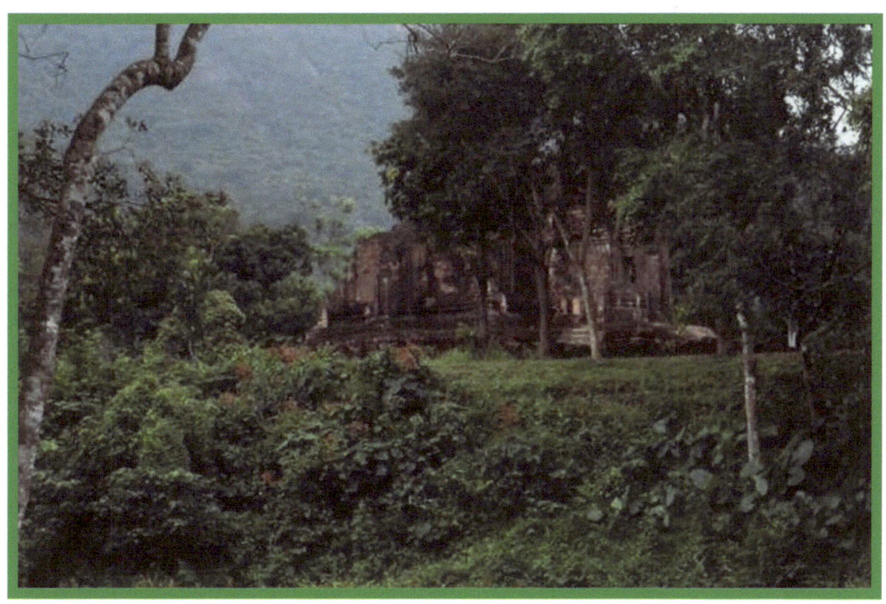

The signs warning visitors to stay on the trails due to unexploded ordnance were a sight that bothered me quite a bit. During my tour in Vietnam, I was an imagery interpreter. My job was to interpret what I thought was on the ground and then to plot the aircraft missions accordingly. I never saw what the actual target looked like on the ground. While visiting this site, I found myself hoping that I was not the one who plotted this mission. The bomb-strike bunkers could be seen everywhere.

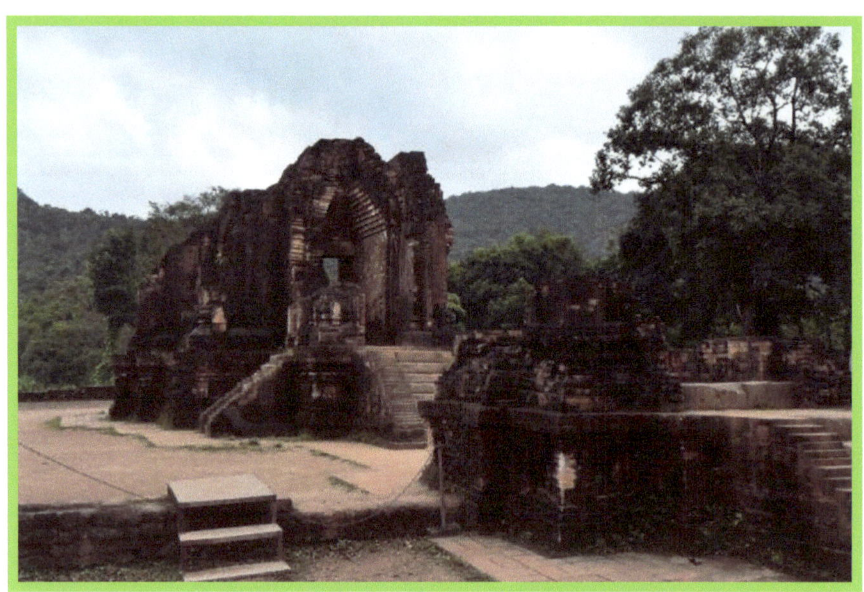

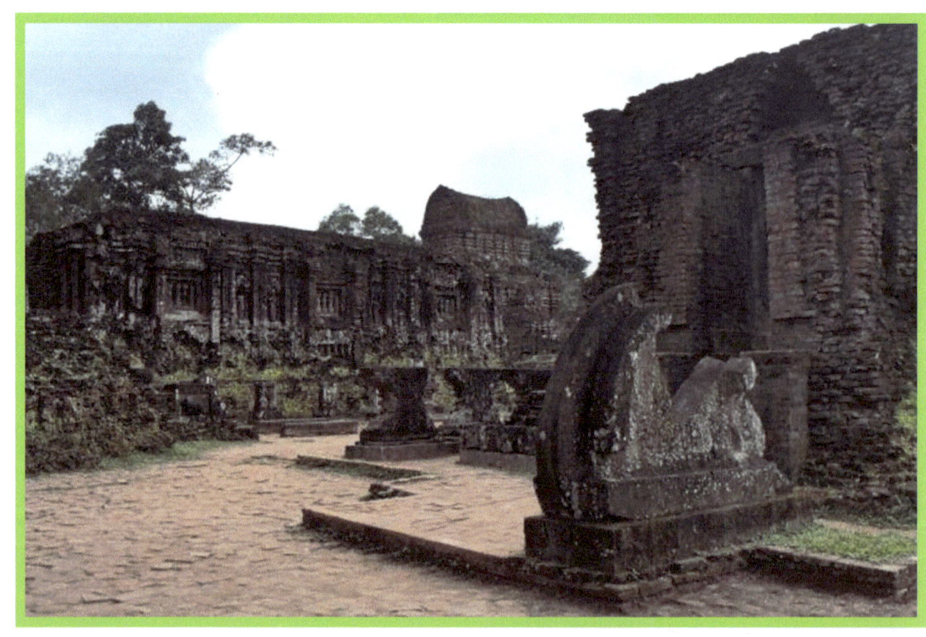

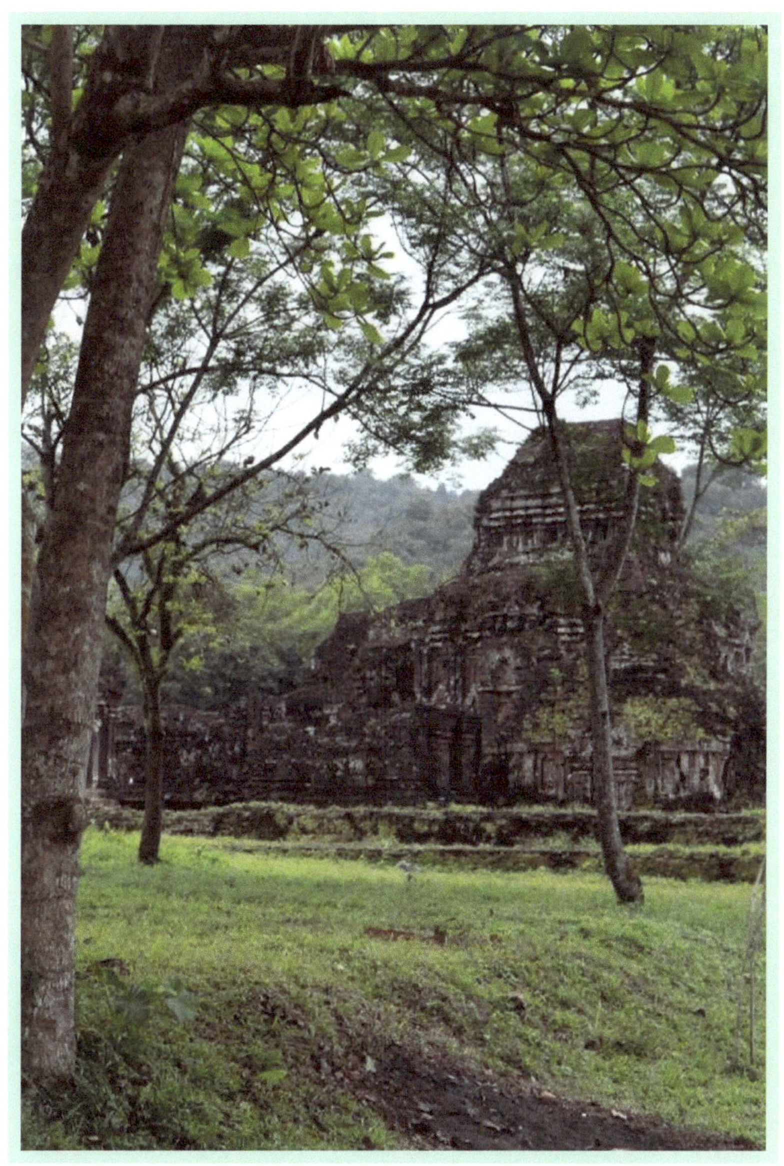

Several paths lead safely into, and around, the ruins. As I walked around this one path by myself, I came upon these Champa dancers. They perform short outdoor performances at different areas of the ruins. This area, known as Cham, was home to Hindus and Muslims and was the Champa empire during ancient times. The cultural dancers were fascinating as they danced with graceful movements to traditional music. The colorful costumes are accessorized in an alluring manner, and the short, dance performances are a highlight of any visit to Vietnam.

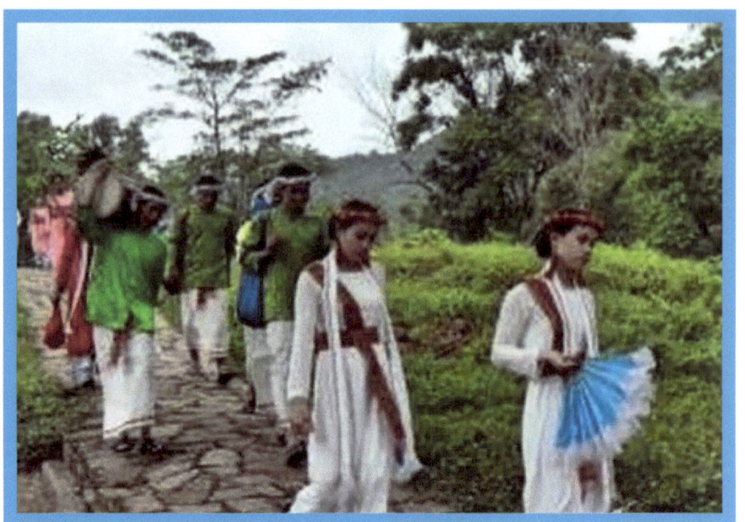

If traveling to My Son alone, be sure you allow plenty of time to explore. To avoid the heat of the day, try visiting during the morning, or evening, hours. Be prepared to do quite a bit of walking around the ruins.

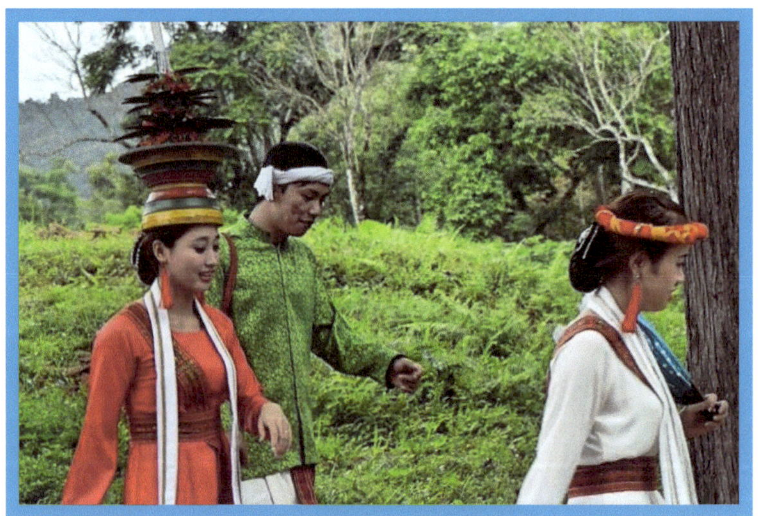

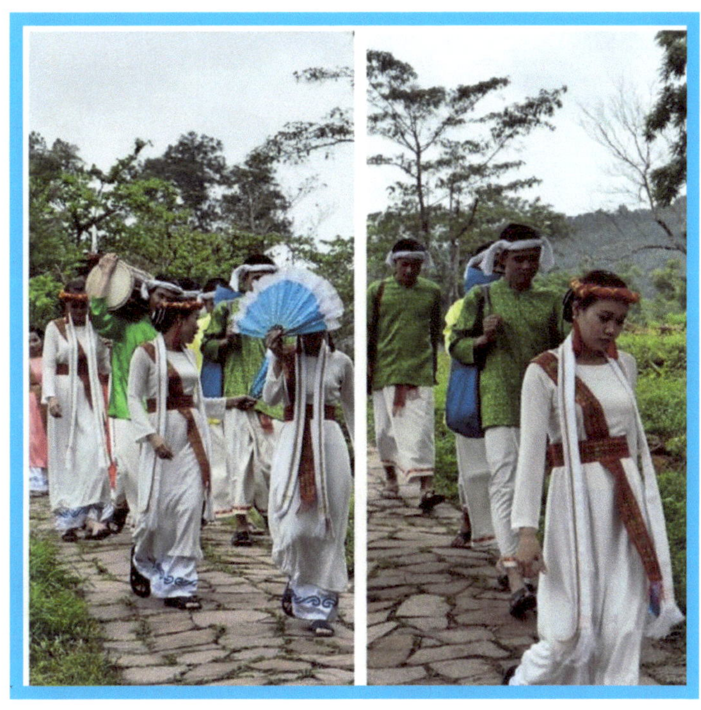

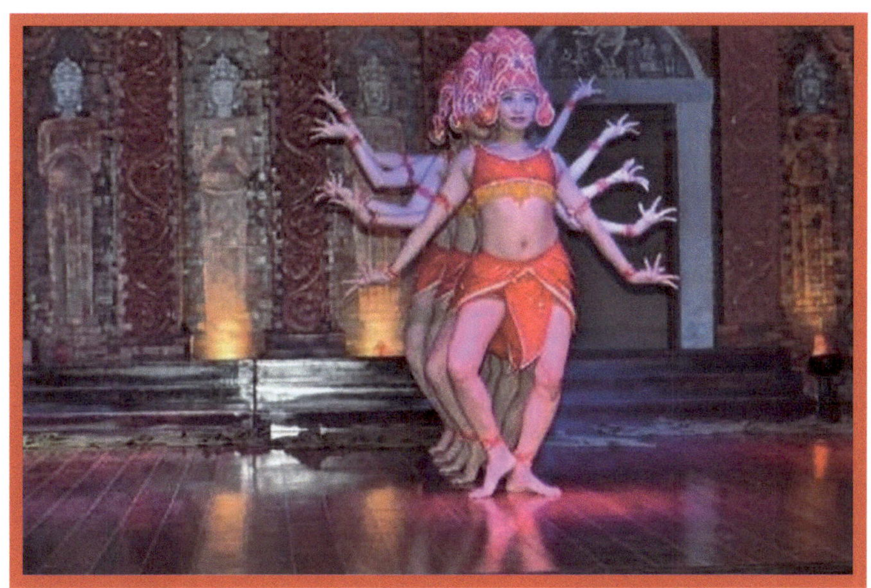

Seeing the dancers perform in their brightly colored costumes against the backdrop of the ruins was a stark and unusual contrast to the decay. Though I was unable to catch any of the outdoor performances amongst the ruins, seeing the dancers on the stage was the highlight of my day.

These dancers perform on stage several times a day, with each performance lasting around 15-20 minutes.

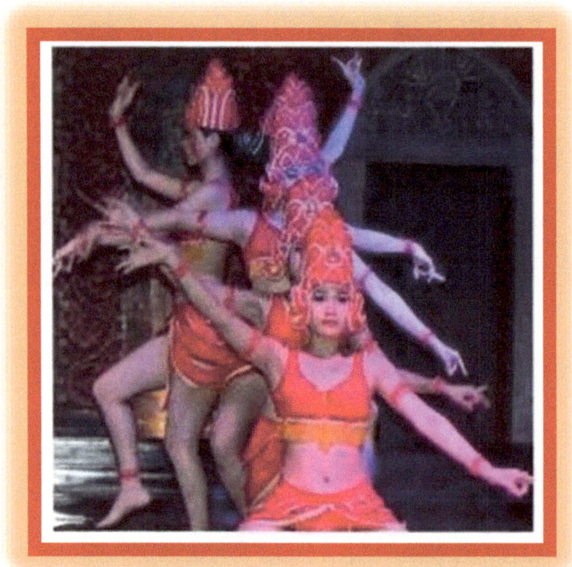

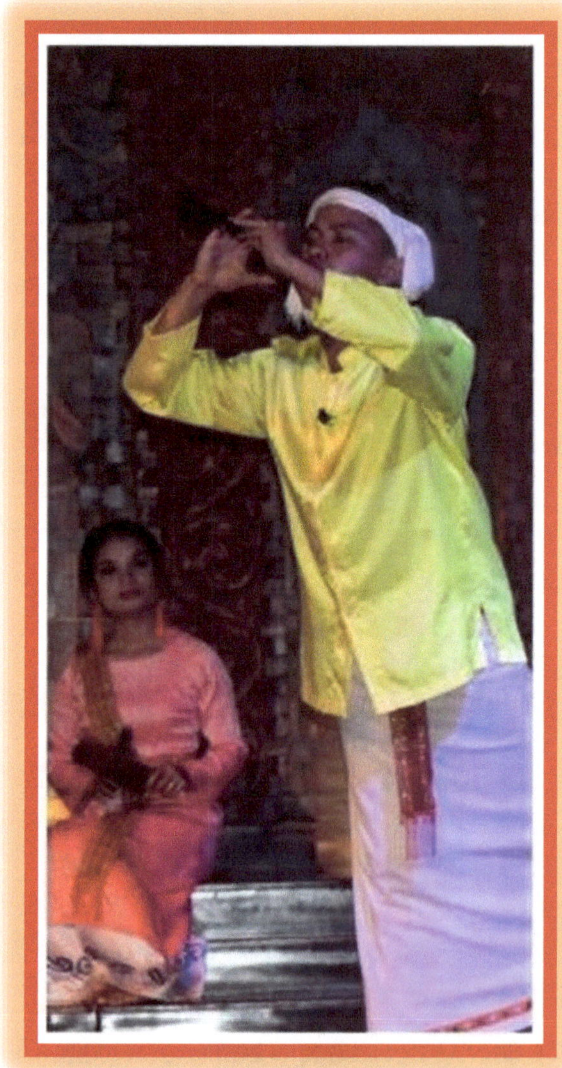

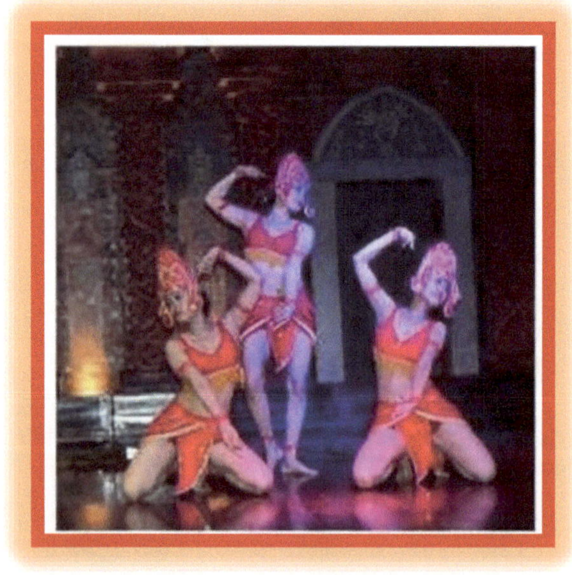

9—Nha Trang

Though it is a short flight from Danang to Nha Trang, the drive time is hours longer. Nah Trang is known, to tourists and locals alike, as the beach capital of Vietnam with its many hotels, bars, restaurants, beautiful beaches, and neighboring islands. "Seafood Capital" might be an equally appropriate name for this city, since fresh fish and shellfish are abundant in this area. Great seafood meals can be found at five-star restaurants, street vendors, and markets alike. During the early morning and evening hours, it was cool enough to enjoy the scenery and local sights while walking along the beach.

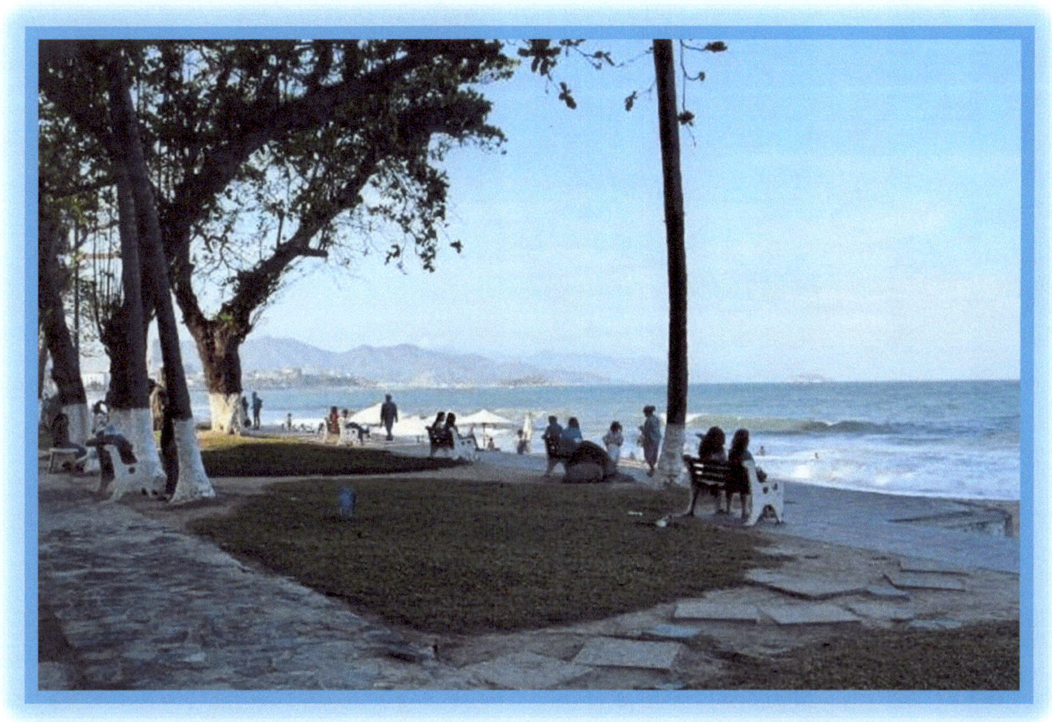

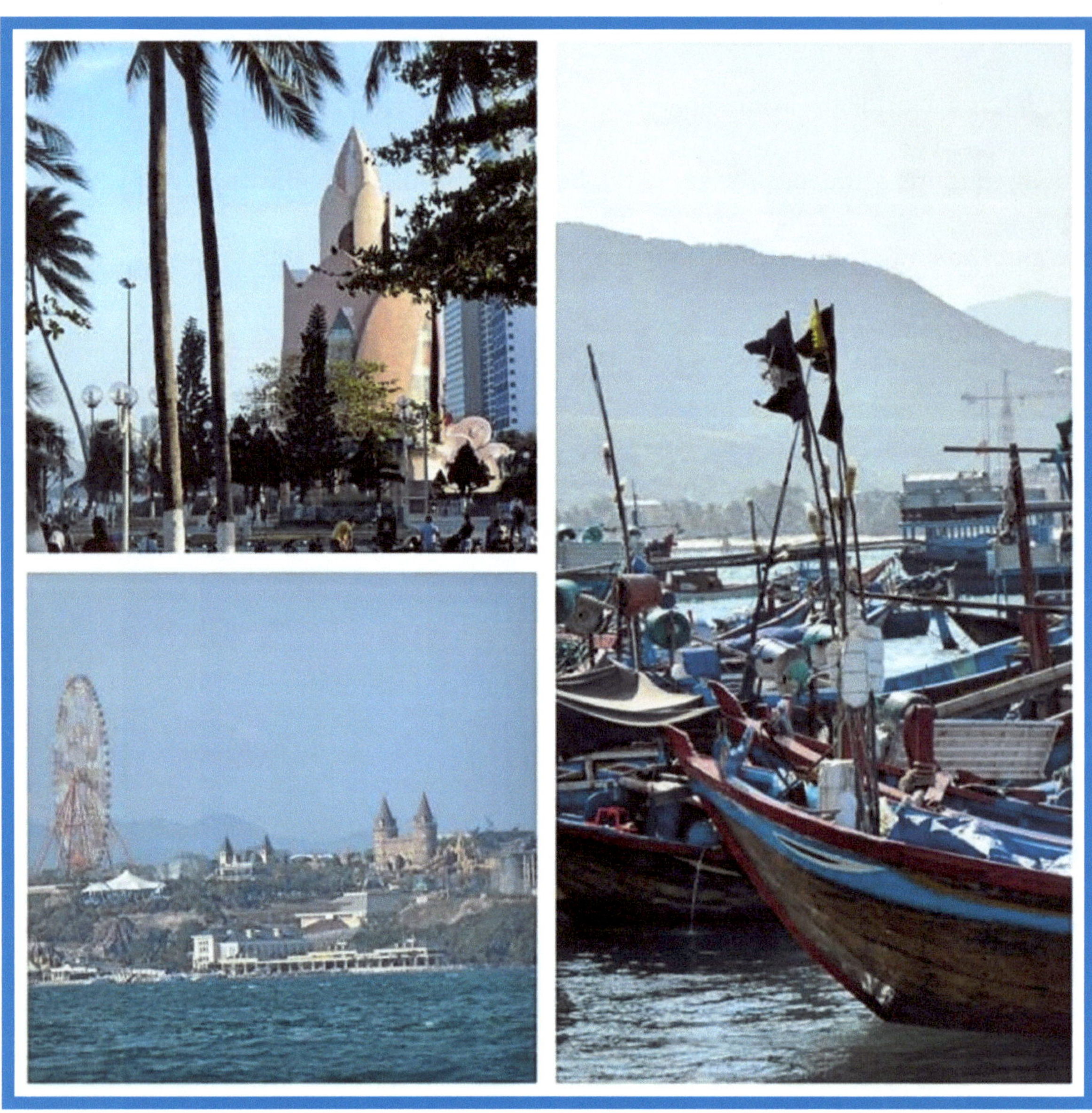

While walking along the beach in Nha Trang, one cannot miss the strikingly pink-colored building shaped like a lotus blossom. This beautiful building is the Thap Huong Museum. It is a featured landmark in the city that also serves as a lighthouse.

During a short boat ride, we caught a glimpse of Vinpearl Nah Trang. Several Vinpearl parks are known as the "Disneyland of Vietnam," though there is no connection to Disneyland. As in our amusement parks, you will encounter long lines, high-priced tickets, and even higher-priced food, however, these parks receive throngs of visitors from all over the world—especially from Asian countries.

While visiting Nha Trang, be sure to grab a round boat ride—or, for that matter, any boat you can find—and go visit some of the rural areas outside of the city. You may be able to discover a family involved in making baskets or chopsticks.

While visiting the family who was making the baskets they, of course, insisted we should try our hand at making the same basket they were making. I should note, there are no pictures of our "product," as our basket-making did not go well. We stopped in to see another family who was busily making chopsticks the old-fashioned way—by hand. It was tedious and hard work, but that is how they had made a living for years.

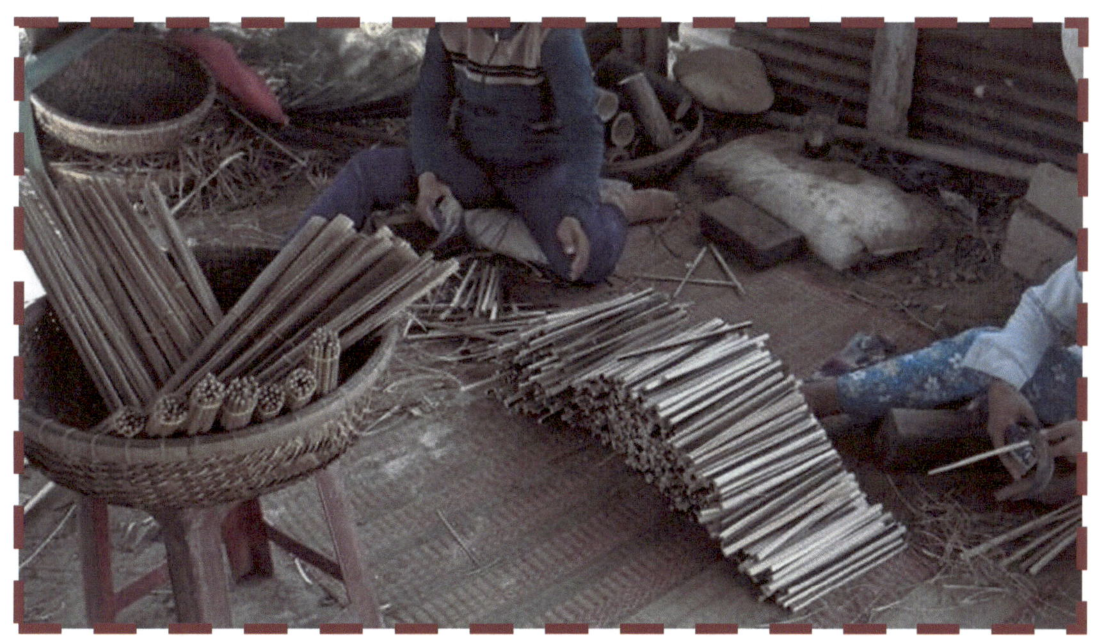

This area is well-known for growing coconut. Coconut products can be found at every roadside stand and vary in style from drinks with a straw poking out to a wide variety of candies and sugars.

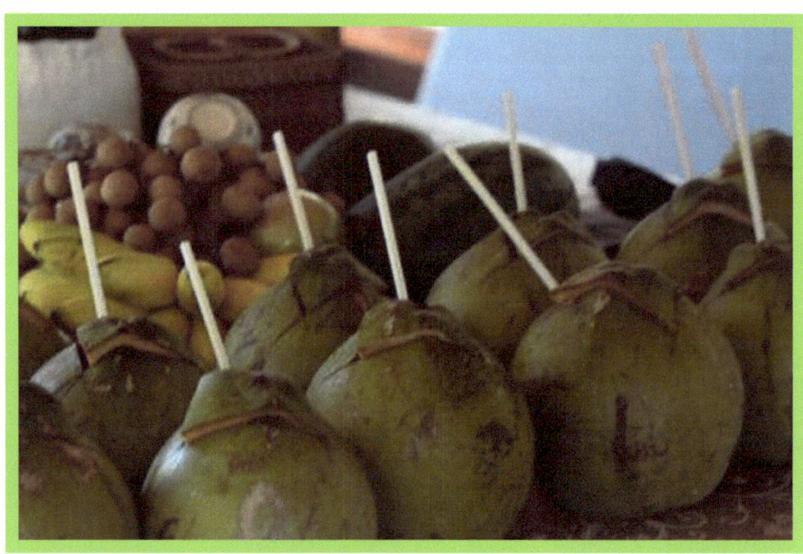

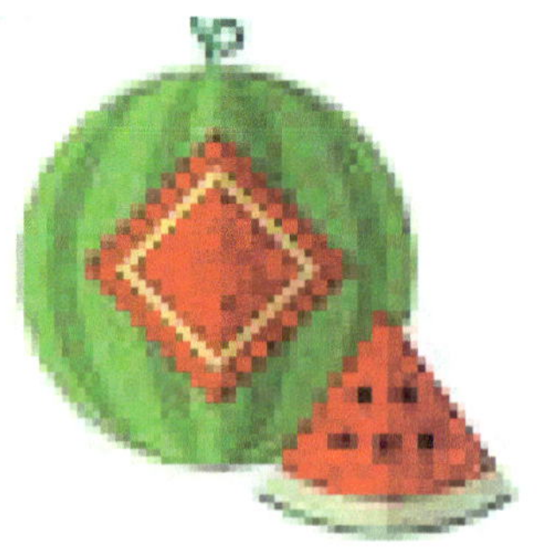

10—Dalat & the Central Highlands

The drive from Nah Trang to Dalat takes you across rice paddies in rural Vietnam and up the mountain into the Central Highlands. Dalat is an agricultural center for flowers and vegetables. Their flowers are shipped all over the world, including to large markets in Europe. There are greenhouses everywhere, many of which were built without any understanding of environmental consequences. Today, many greenhouses are being replaced with a more sensitive approach to the environment and sustainable agriculture.

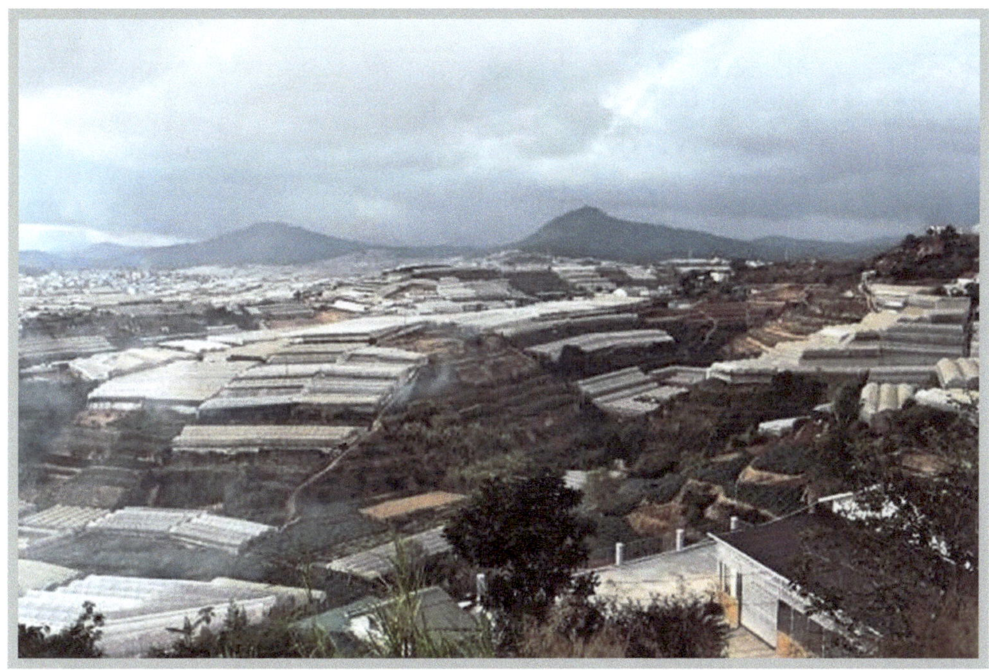

Someone who has lived in Dalat for most of his life told us there were an estimated 40,000 greenhouses in the area at the height of their construction. Stores and markets are loaded with locally grown vegetables. Some markets sell every type of flower available in the greenhouses. I enjoy visiting a market at every stop just to see the differences in the produce of each area we visit.

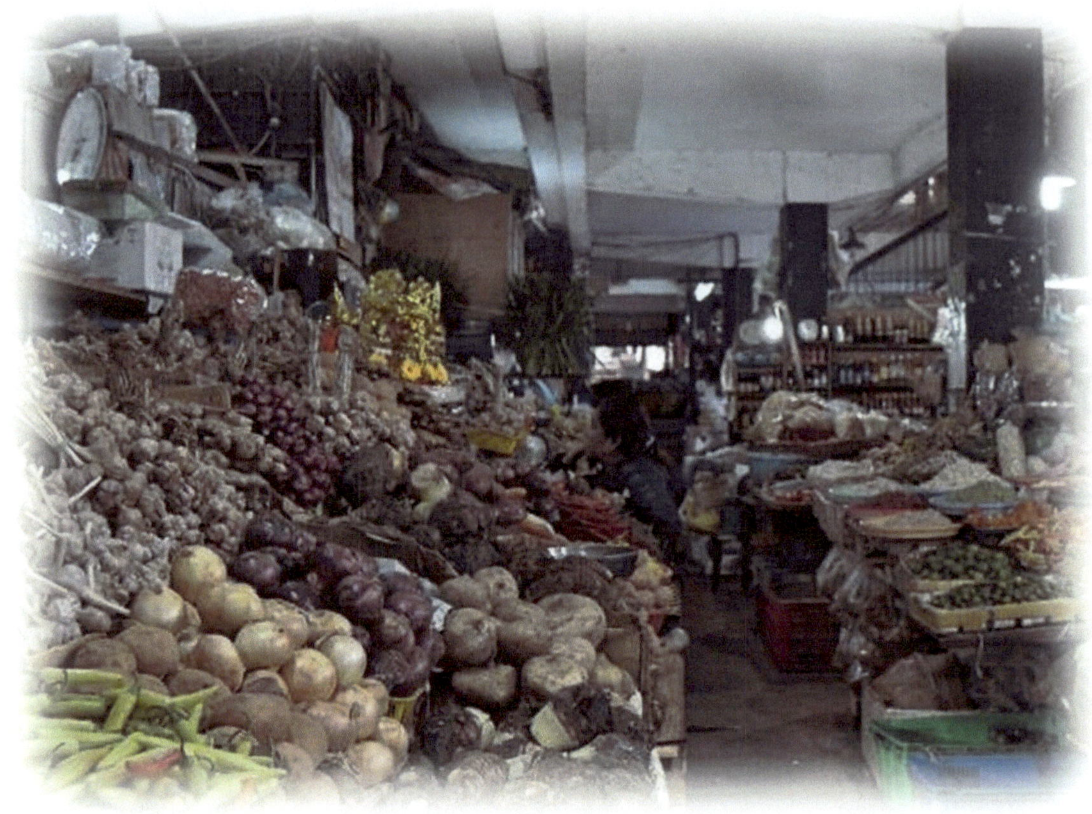

I have already mentioned how enjoyable it is to get out and walk to places of interest, provided the humidity and heat are not unbearable. One cloudy afternoon I took off walking toward a lake and park near a downtown area in Dalat that was not far from my hotel. The nice thing about these walks is discovering something new along the way. Sometimes it is something extraordinary—like the traffic circle I had to cross that day. It was unexpected and rather whimsical. Its amazing design was made up of a beautiful work of art complete with flowers, wire, and a vivid imagination.

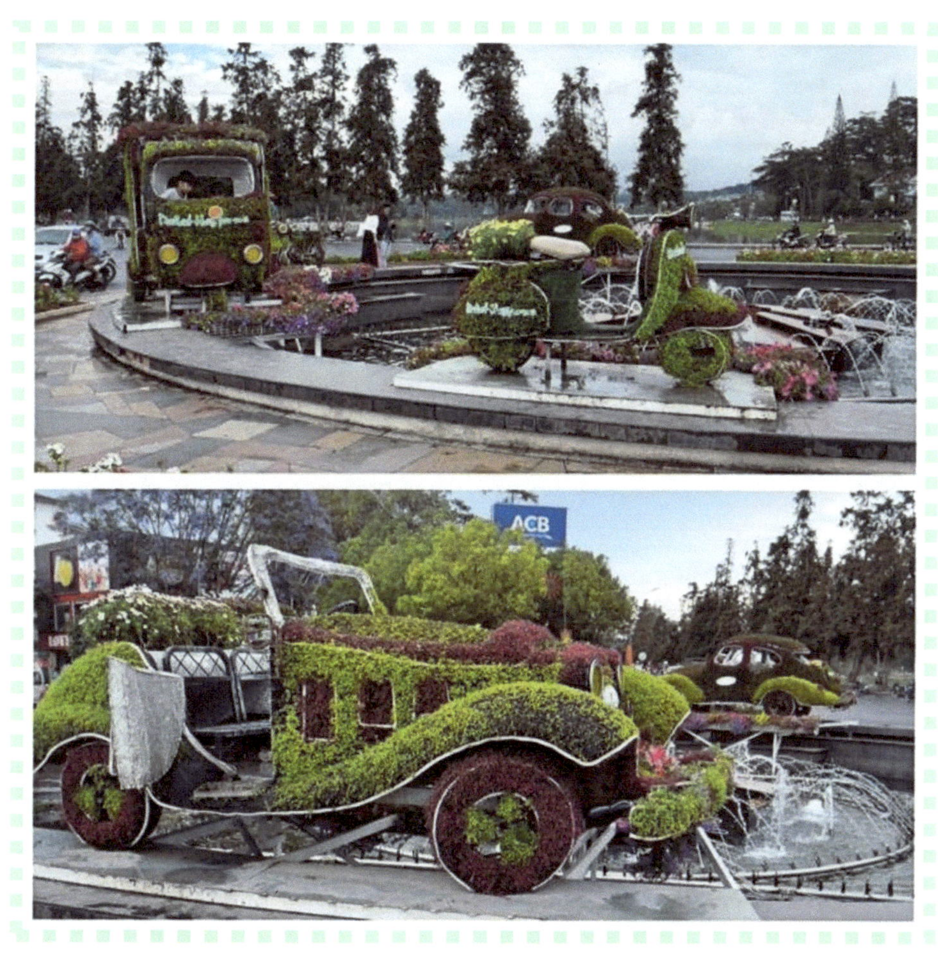
ACB

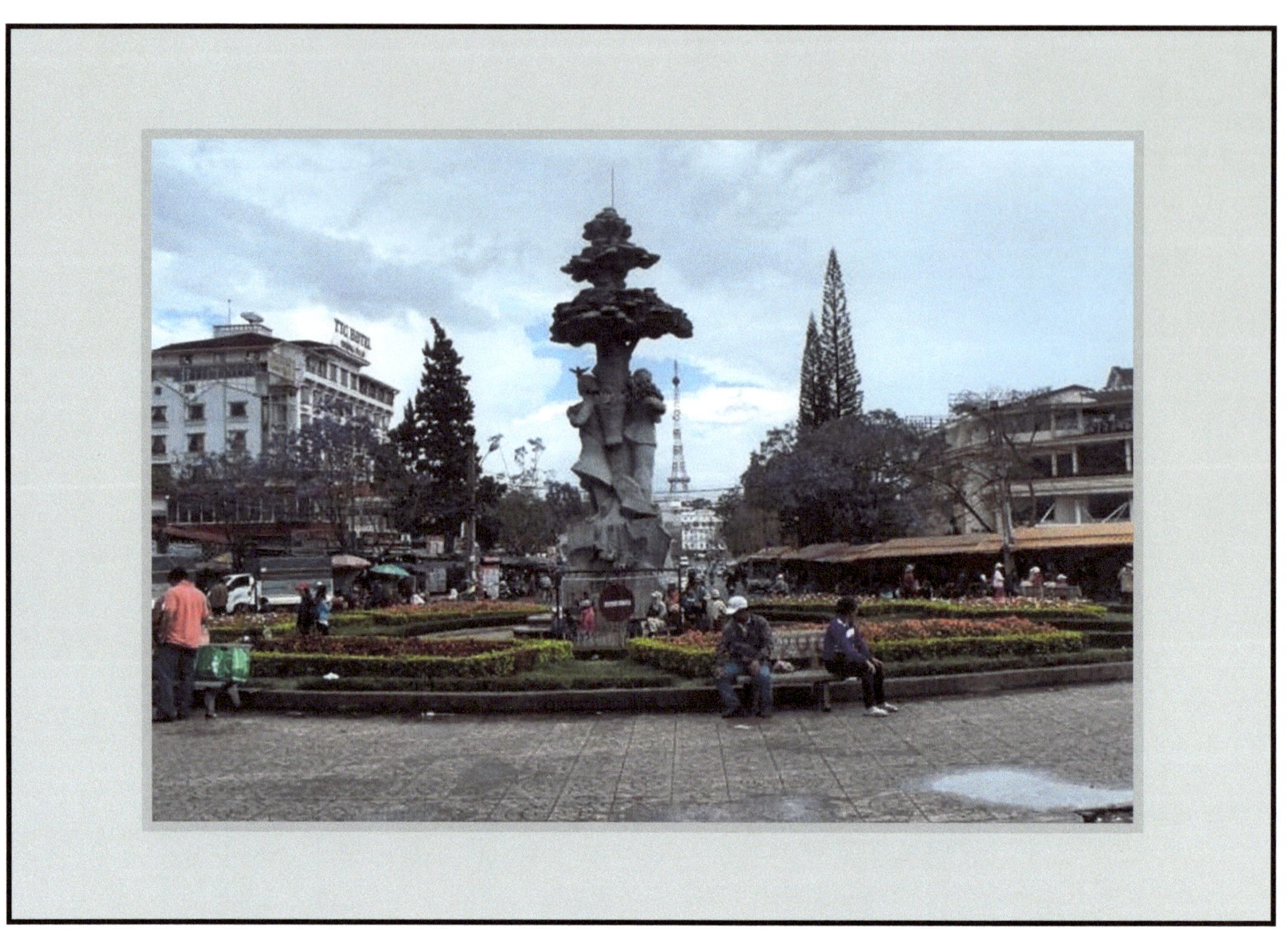

It seems no matter where I travel around the world, I always see and learn something out of the ordinary. This trip was no exception. Traveling outside of Dalat to another part of the central highlands, we visited a remote village where subsistence living and family operations are normal. It is here I was exposed to something I had never heard of—weasel poop coffee. And yes, it is exactly as it sounds.

Weasels are kept in cages and are fed ripe coffee fruits—or cherries, as they are called. Once the fruit is pooped out, it is recovered, cleaned, and then roasted. Supposedly, the weasels have picky palates and only consume the fruit that is untainted by disease or is otherwise deemed less than worthy by the picky eater. Researchers have concluded that the enzymes produced during the weasel's digestive process alter the chemical character of the cherry. The coffee producer we visited made sure to offer us a cup of their weasel poop coffee.

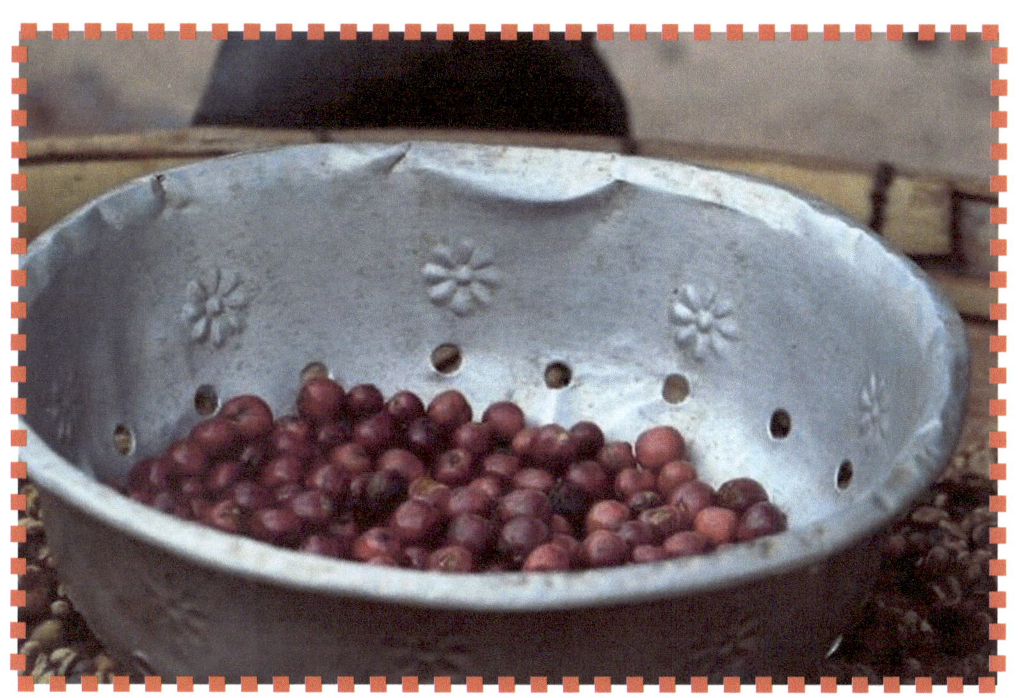

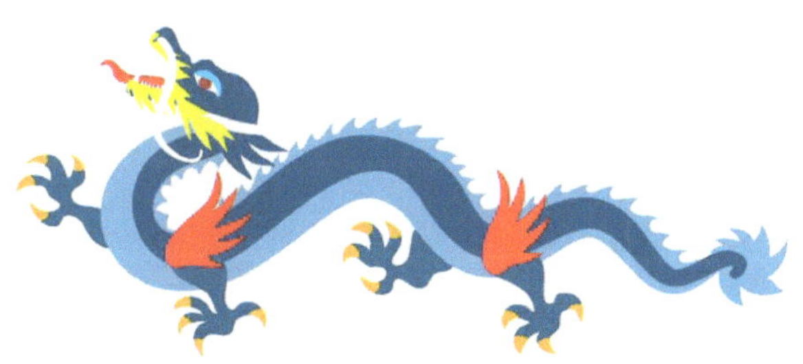

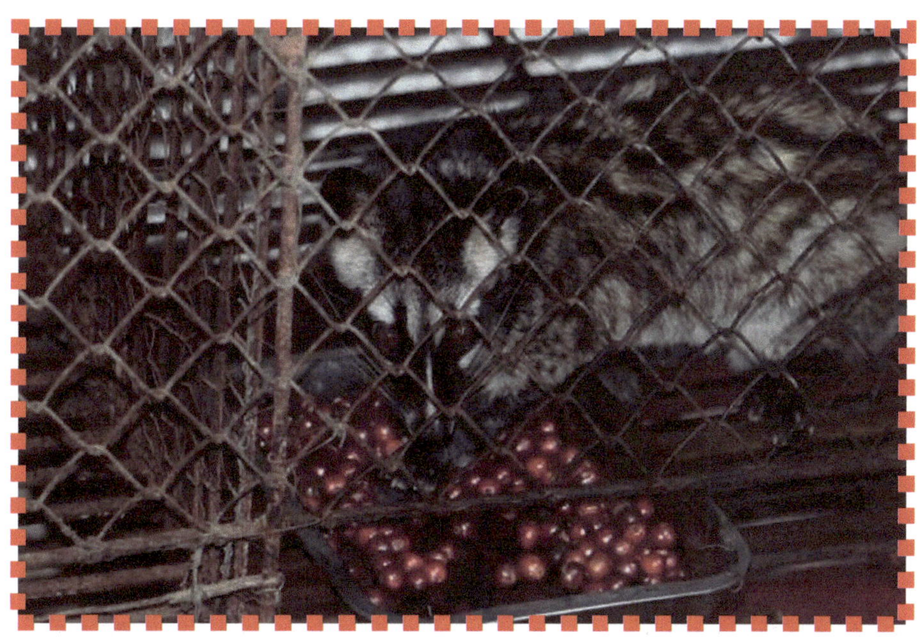

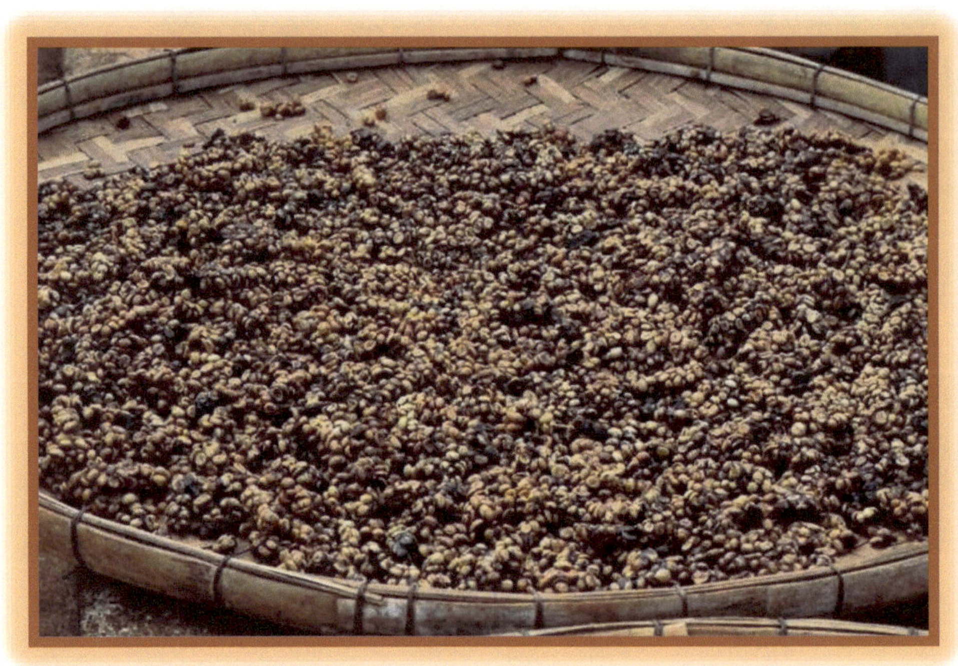

Of course, we all had to try a cup of this strange coffee which is thought, by many, to be the most expensive in the world selling for as much as $3,500 per kilo and higher. I have read that one can go into an upscale coffee house in London and expect to pay 50 pounds per cup. I found it to be OK coffee. Nothing extraordinary when compared to my favorite back home.

We visited the village of Buon Chuoi, also known as the banana village. It is an isolated village accessible only by sitting on a trailer that is pulled up the hill by a tractor. The villagers are K'ho Chil, better known by most as "Montagnard," which encompasses dozens of different, central highland, tribal entities. While there, we visited the schools and saw how the villagers worked to survive. Many of these tribes were placed in government-built communities under the watchful eye of the reunified government as the Montagnard supported the South and aided American soldiers during the war. The relocation settlements can still be seen, though most sit empty today.

The road to the village is very narrow, limiting village access. A rich, volcanic soil called "laterite" paints the road and hillside a reddish hue. If you are ever caught in a rainstorm or dry windstorm on this soil your clothes will forever be stained this reddish color. It is very difficult to remove the soil from clothing.

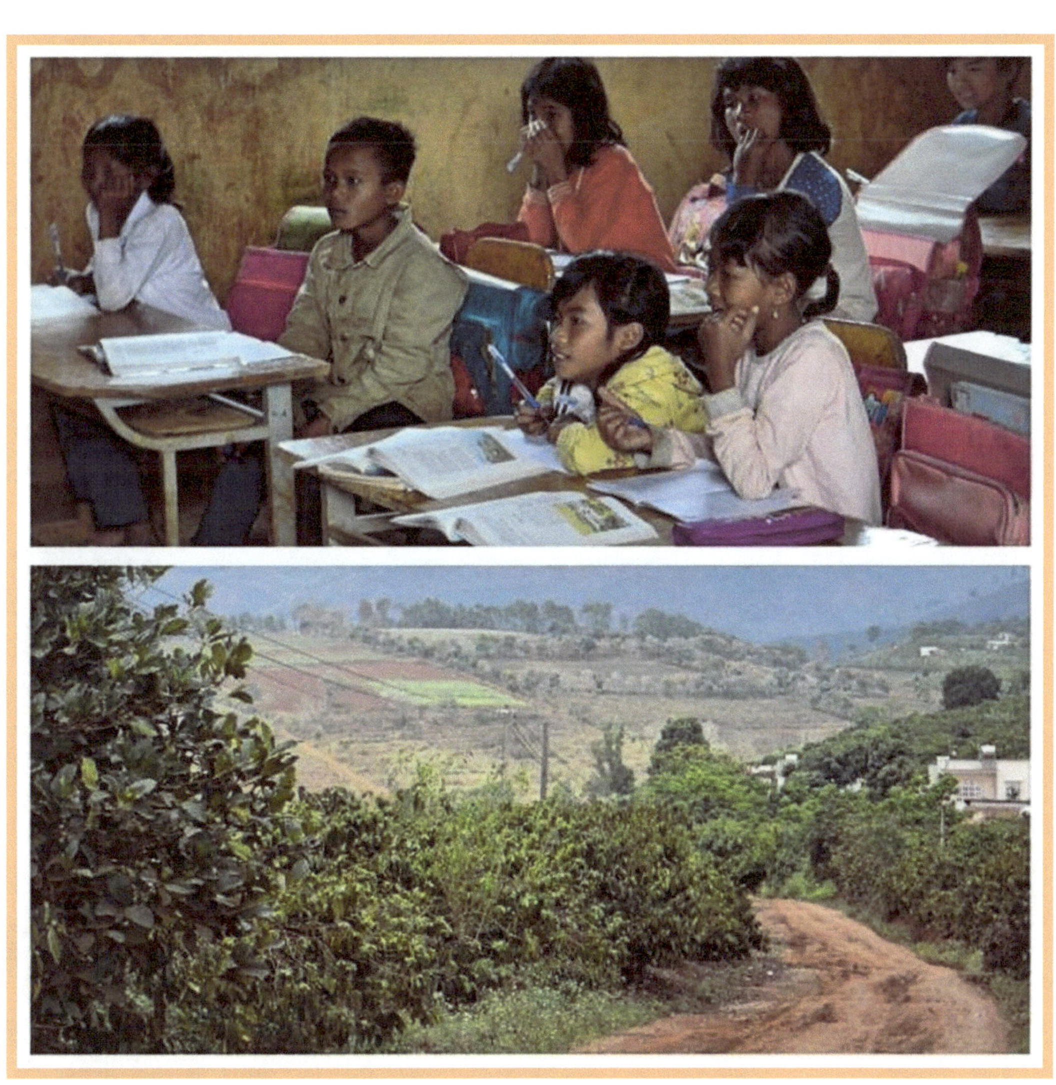

While there, we visited the children's school and walked around the village. Though it looks like a poor village, the hills surrounding it show just how fertile and rich the soil is, providing the villagers with almost everything they need.

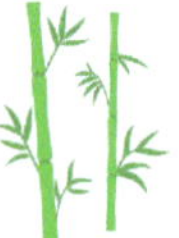

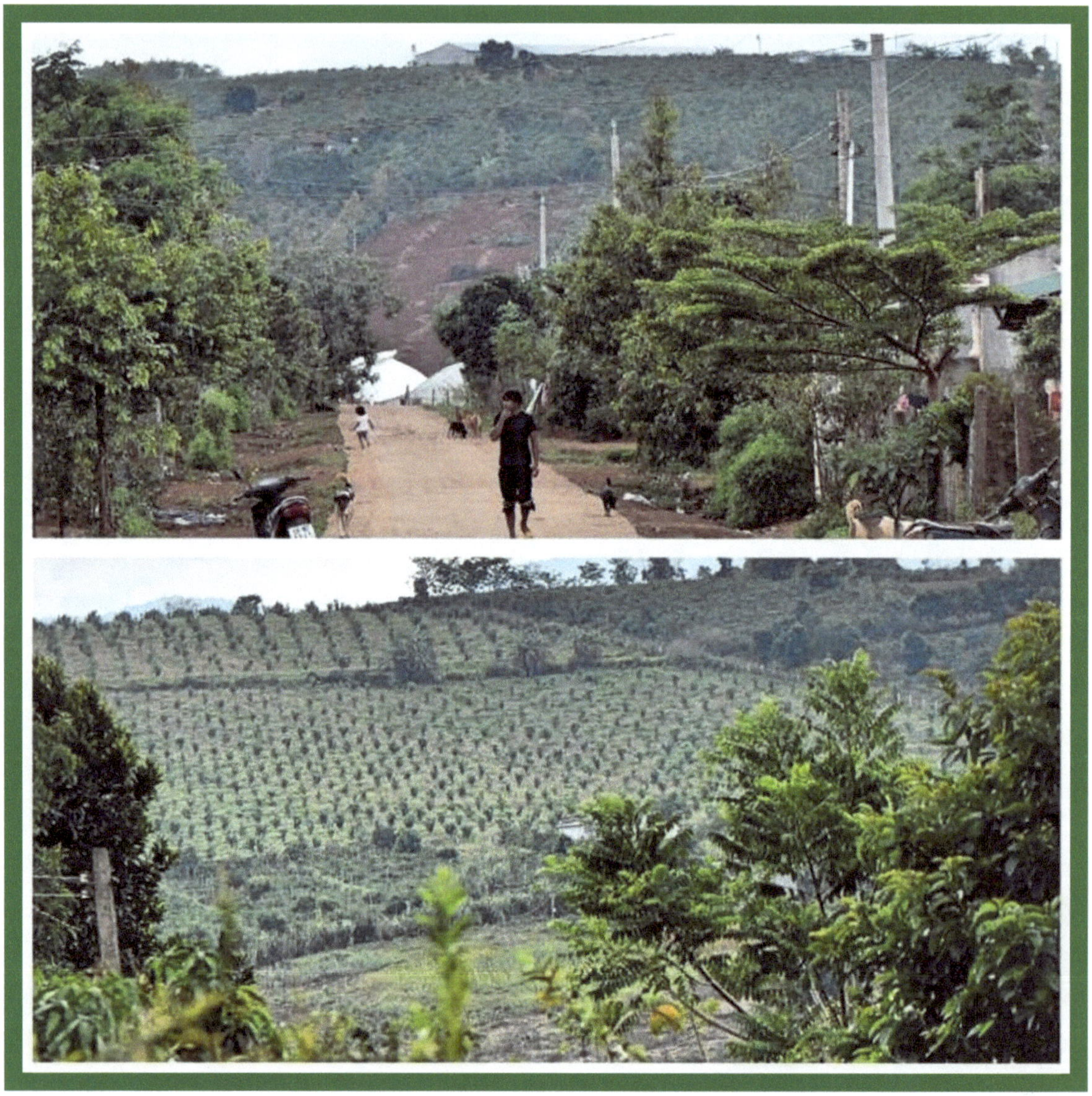

The children who did not attend school followed us everywhere we went, giggling, laughing, and posing for pictures. This woman allowed us to take a picture with her two daughters. She appeared to be a happy mother with two, healthy, bright-eyed daughters.

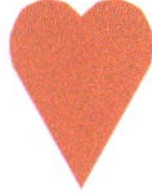

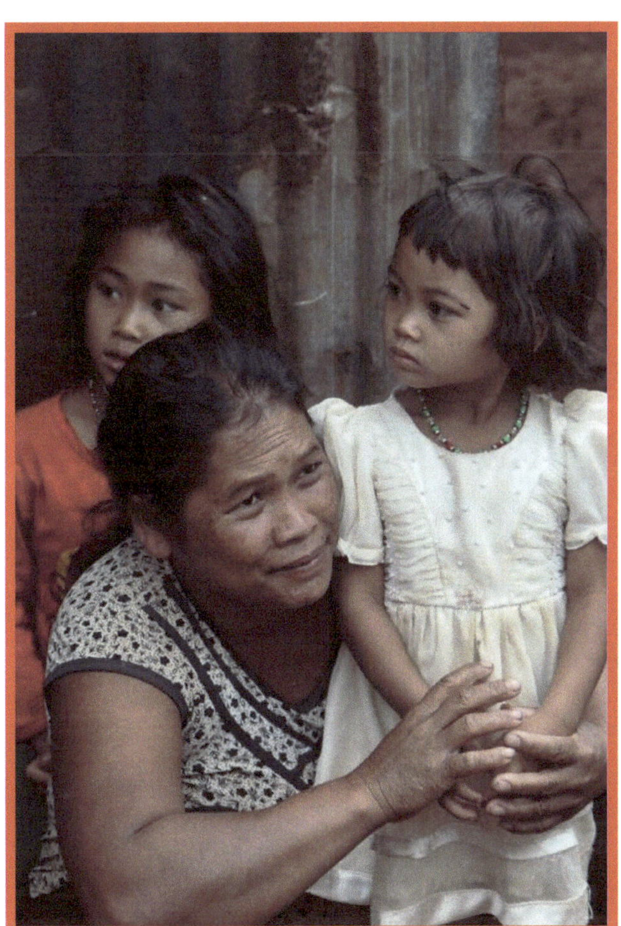

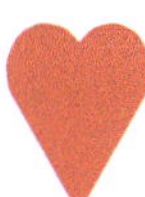

When you are in Dalat, leave plenty of time to visit the Dalat railway station and ride the cog rail line. In the past, it ran from Dalat to Thap Cham, which was 84 km away. Due to attacks by the Viet Cong, it ceased operation in 1964. Today it runs as a 30-minute ride to the town of Trai Mat. As you wander through the fertile countryside of family-owned terraces and see the small gardens that grow everything from fruits and vegetables to herbs and flowers of all types, you will find that Trai Mat is well worth the ride.

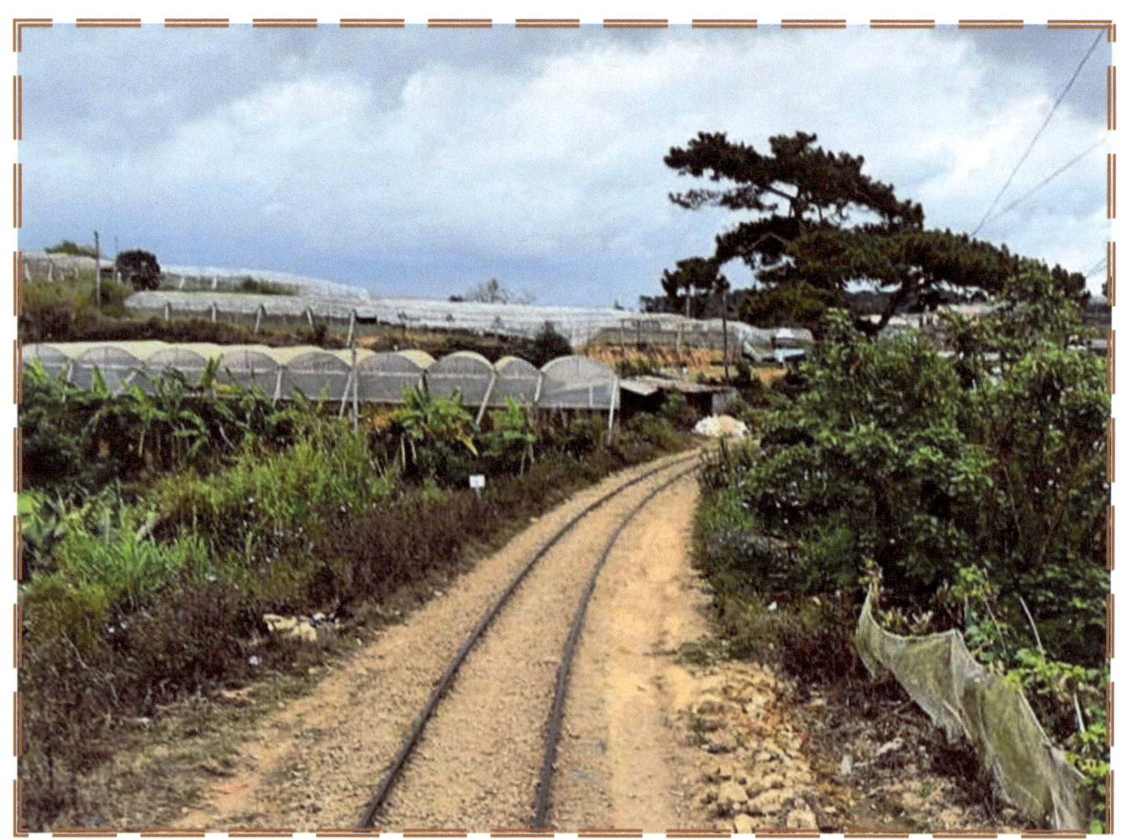

The beautiful Linh Phuoc Pagoda is the main attraction for most who visit Trai Mat. A modern pagoda built between 1949 and 1952, it is one of the most unusual and unique Buddhist temples I have visited. In the temple's glass exterior inlays a wide variety of colors is on display. In addition, there is a variety of terracotta tiles as well as beautiful porcelain. Nearby are several places to eat and many souvenir shops. This important temple is of religious significance to many visitors from around the world and is usually crowded. Despite the crowds, you should allow yourself plenty of time to climb the stairs, tour the interior, and admire the exterior from whatever vantage point suits you.

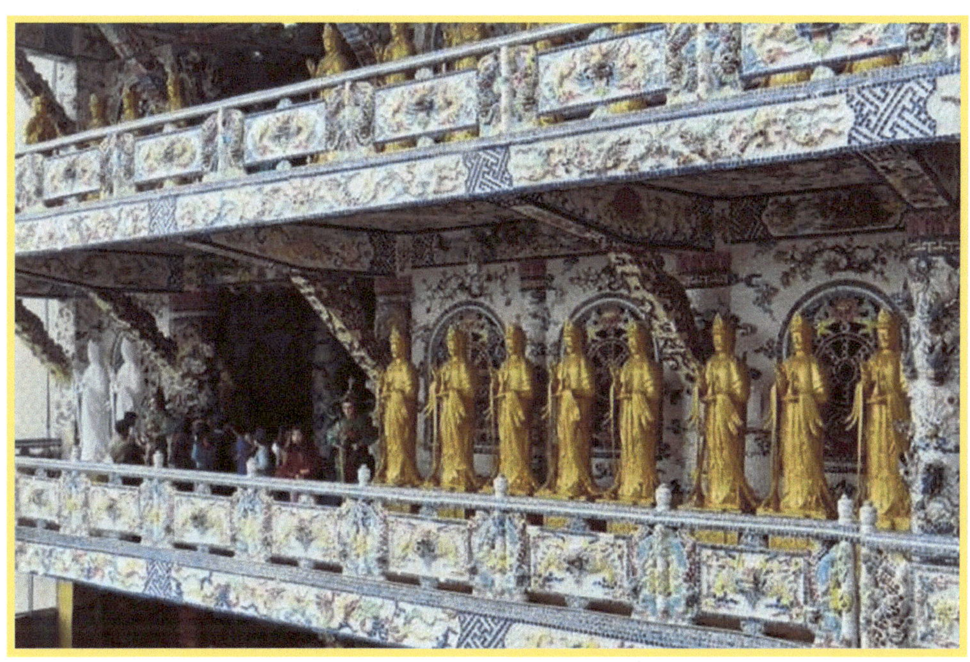

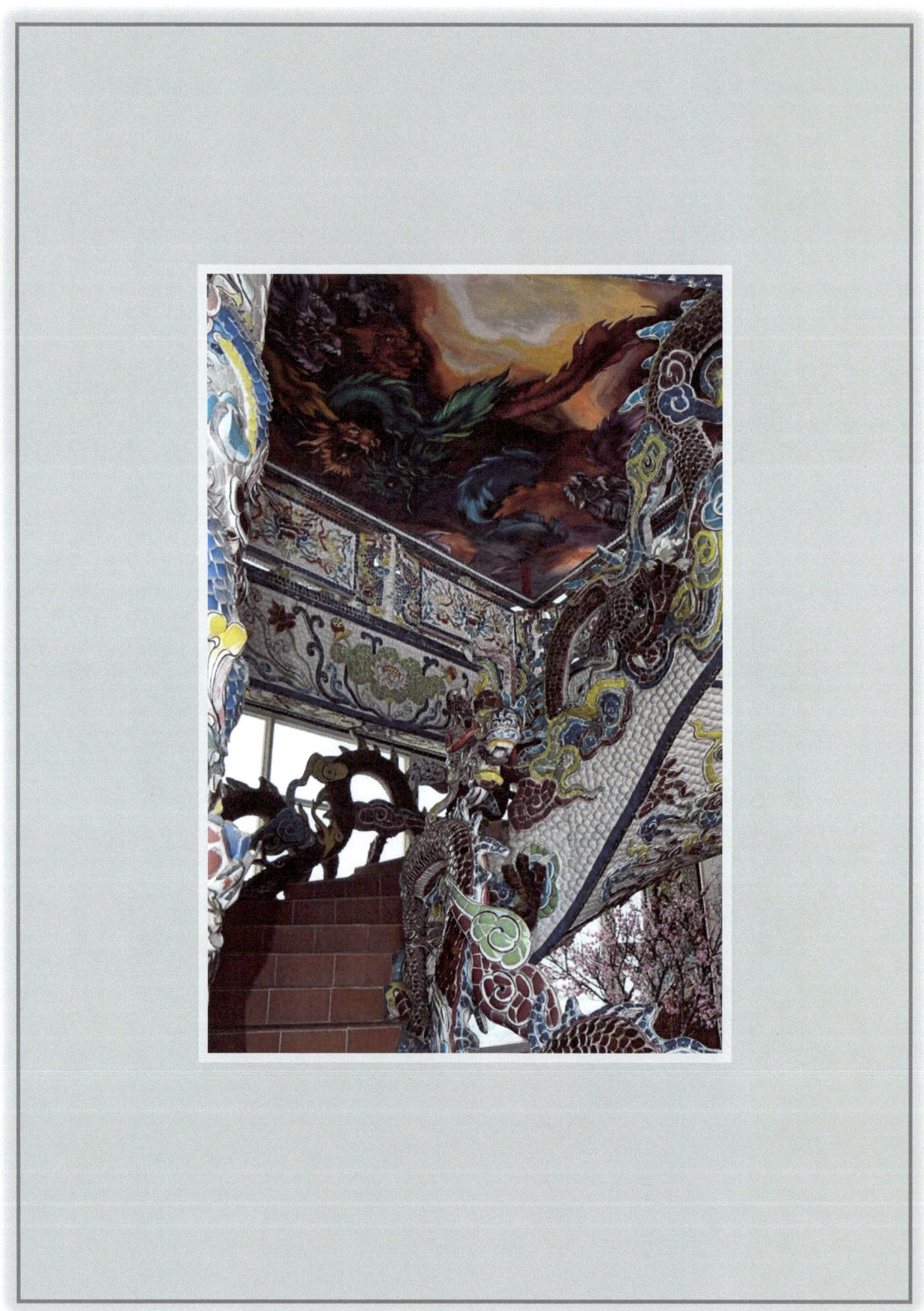

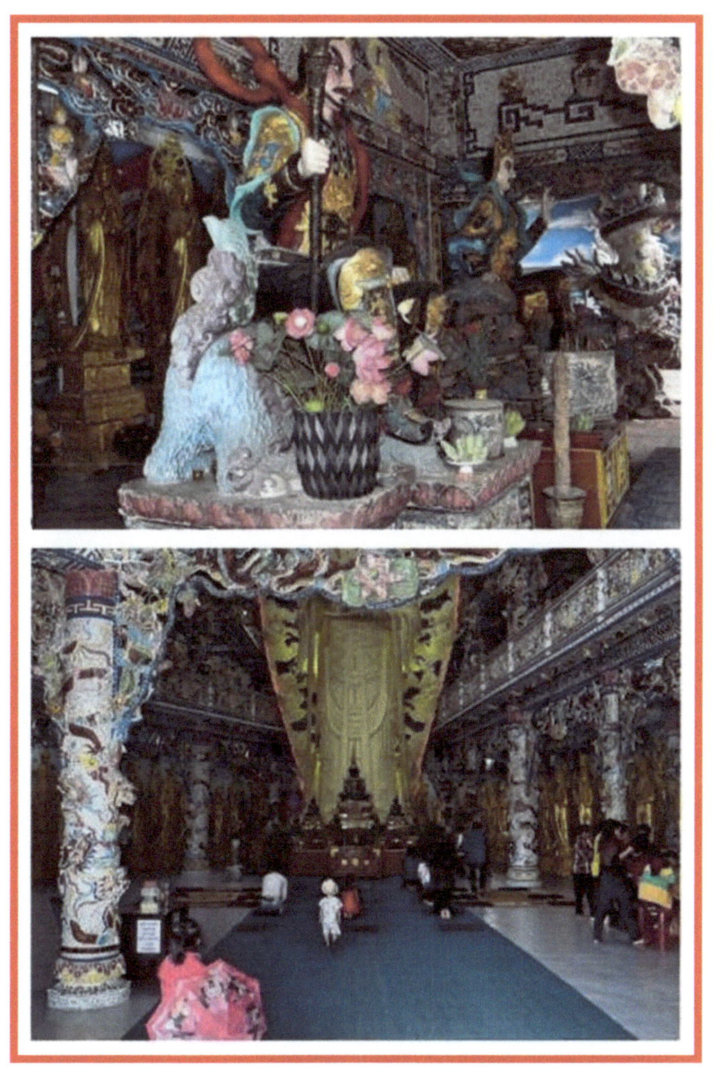

As you can see, the temple is colorful, artistic, and well worth your time.

After our time in Dalat, we will head further south to Ho Chi Minh City (Saigon) and will follow the Mekong River into the delta region.

11—The Mekong River & Delta

After the fall of the south, Saigon's name was changed to Ho Chi Minh City in honor of the person who sought independence from the French in 1945. I still refer to the city as Saigon since that is how I knew it over 50 years ago. Many who live in the south, and some from other areas, prefer to call it Saigon as well. When I was sent to Saigon, after being drafted into the Army, my workstation was near Thon Son Nhut Airbase, which is now the international airport. Our unit lived in a small compound about six km southeast of the city.

Our compound was near the Saigon River which flows into another river and ends up in the South China Sea. The major river of the area—on which we traveled to its delta—is, of course, the Mekong. The Mekong River is one of the world's largest rivers. It flows from China through Myanmar (Burma), Laos, Thailand Cambodia, and, finally, through Vietnam into the South China Sea. The total length is just under 5,000 kilometers. Outside of Saigon, I enjoyed traveling to the area around Ben Tre and being on the banks, or even *on*—the Mekong River. While there, I experienced the wide variety of products that are dependent upon the river.

There are numerous fishing boats of every size, shape, and age working the river system. Along the shore are numerous villages, many of which are worth visiting. Many of the families that depend on the river for their livelihood either live on the river or next to it.

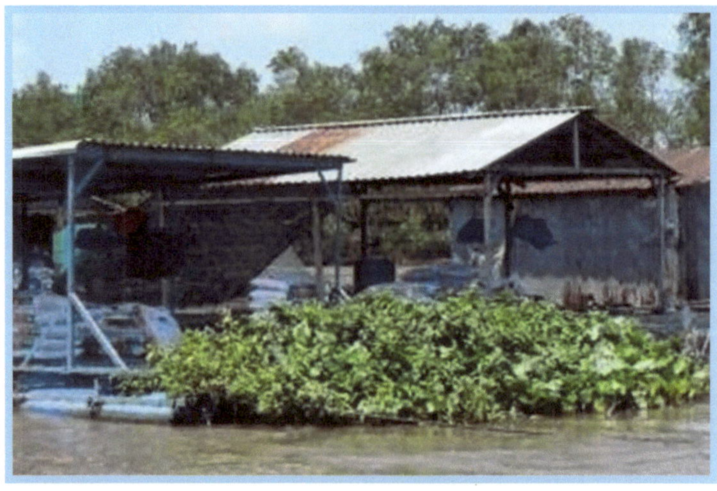

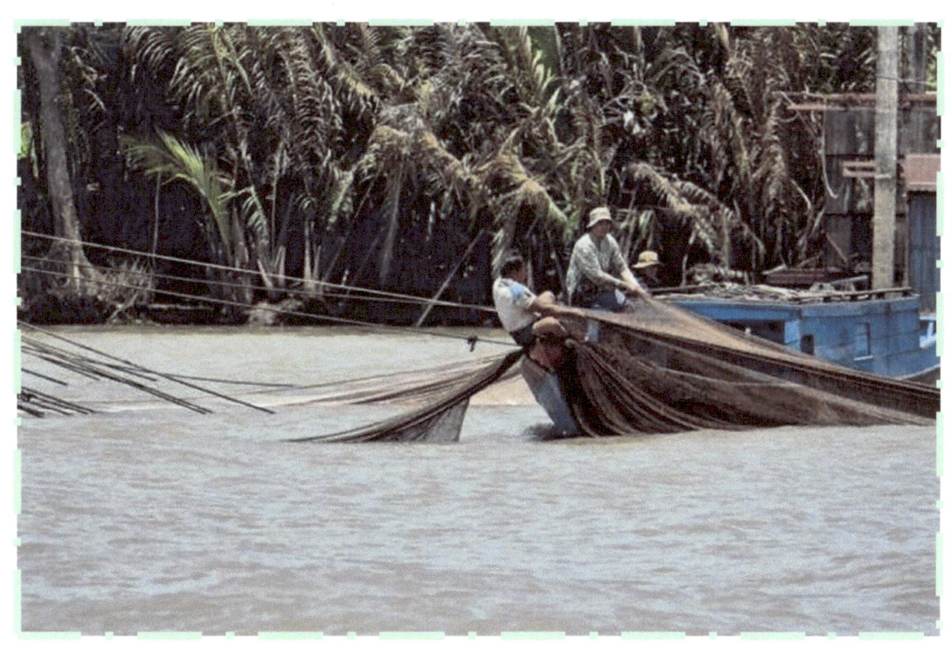

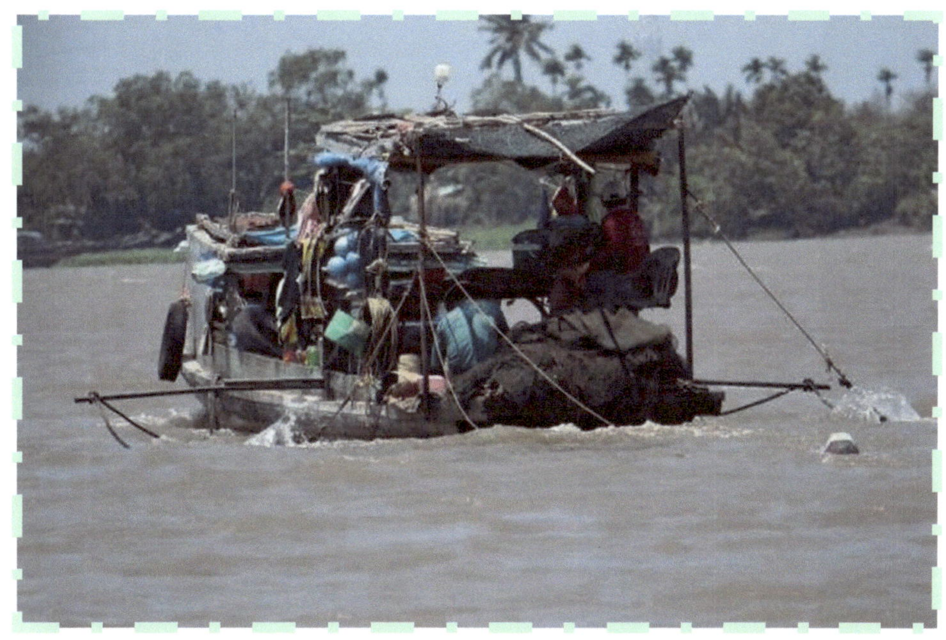

The land surrounding Ben Tre is known for its coconut plantations, which are spread out over the entire area, as well as for its extensive rice fields that lie between numerous canals and smaller rivers. Offshore, there are several small islands to visit. A large percentage of the province could be lost to climate change and the rising seas due to Ben Tre and its extensive irrigation system of canals. Half of this province is only around four feet above sea level, and any rise in sea levels could be disastrous.

Several local guides can take you to any of the canals that are in the area. It is a worthwhile way to spend a few hours on the water.

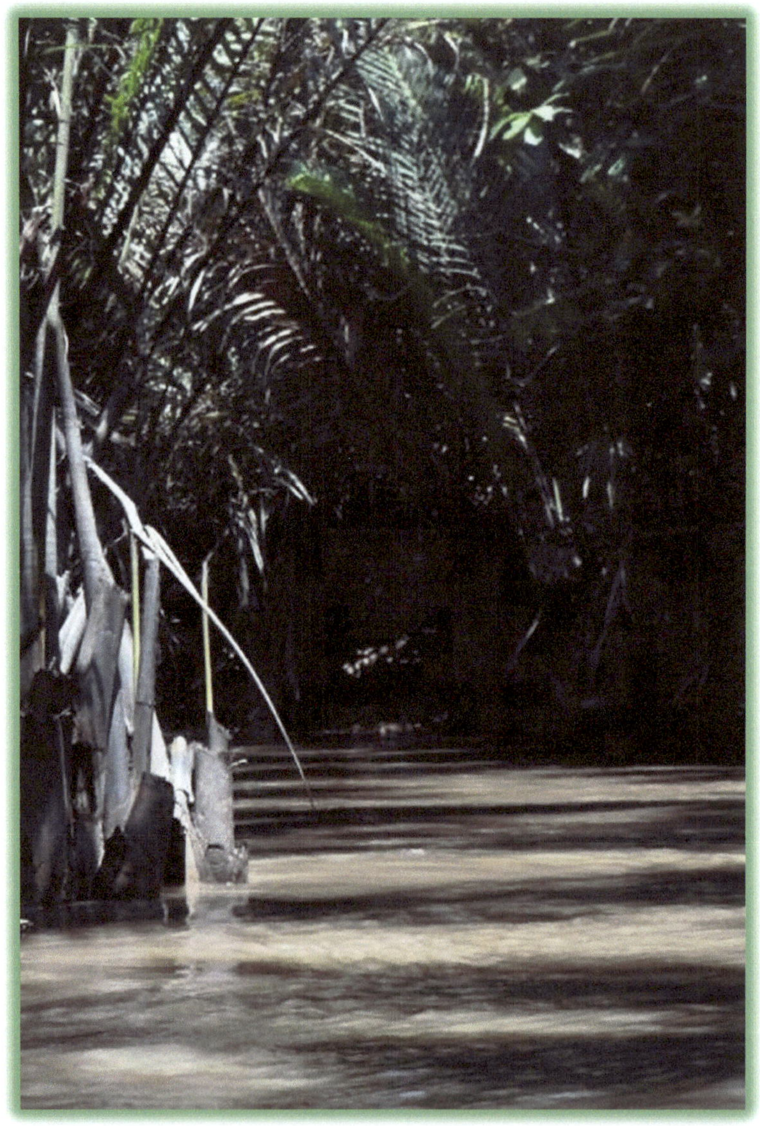

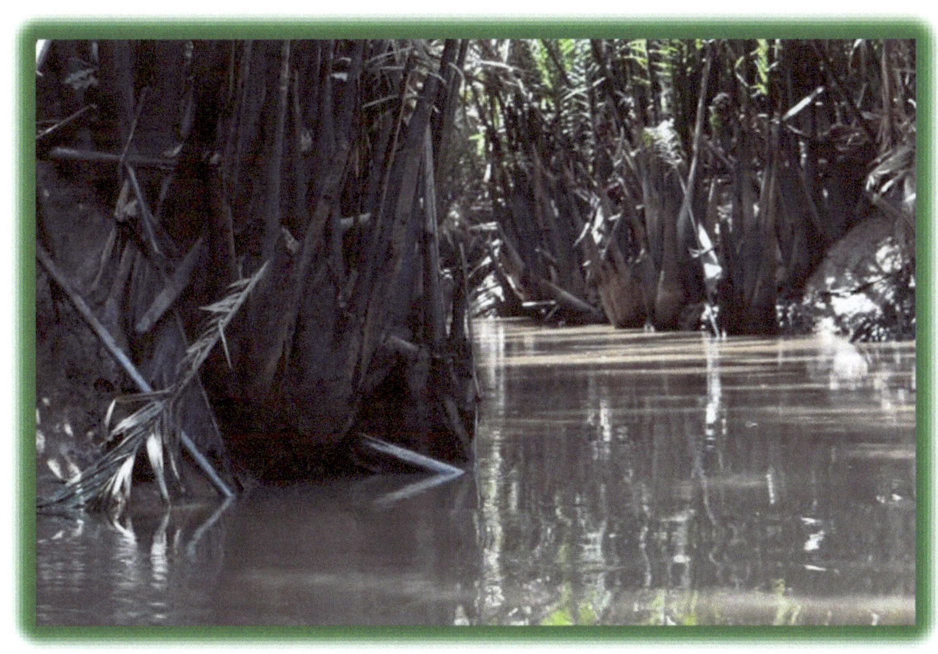

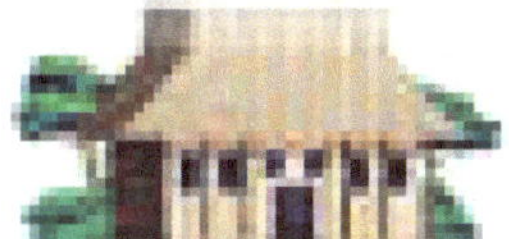

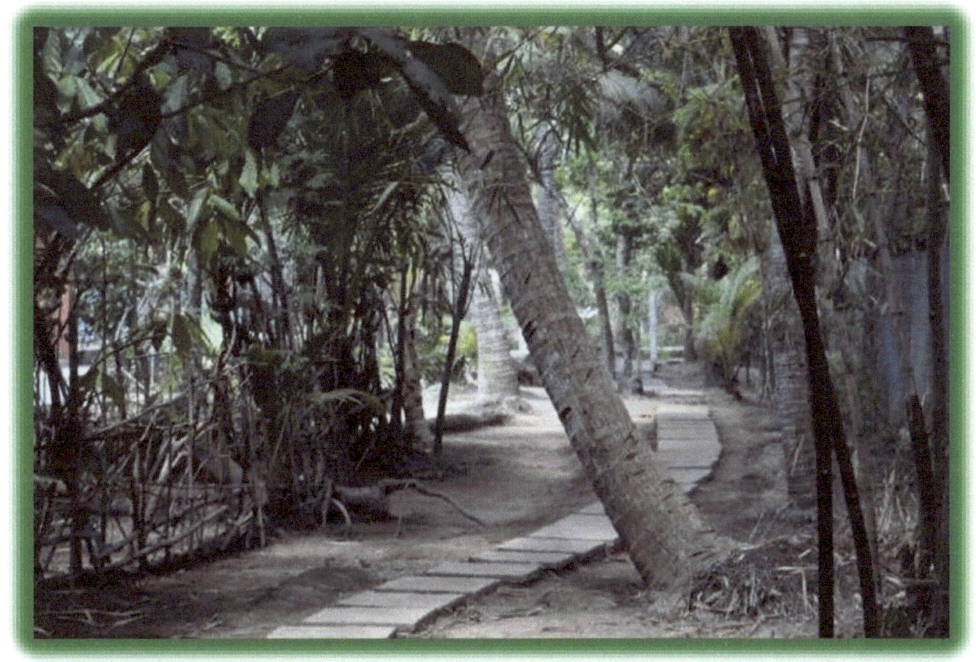

If a boat ride through one of the canals or smaller rivers does not catch your interest, perhaps a walk through the coconut or banana plantations would. While out on a short walk, we saw first-hand the production of a chewy coconut candy known as "keo dua" at a family operation that had been producing candy by hand for years.

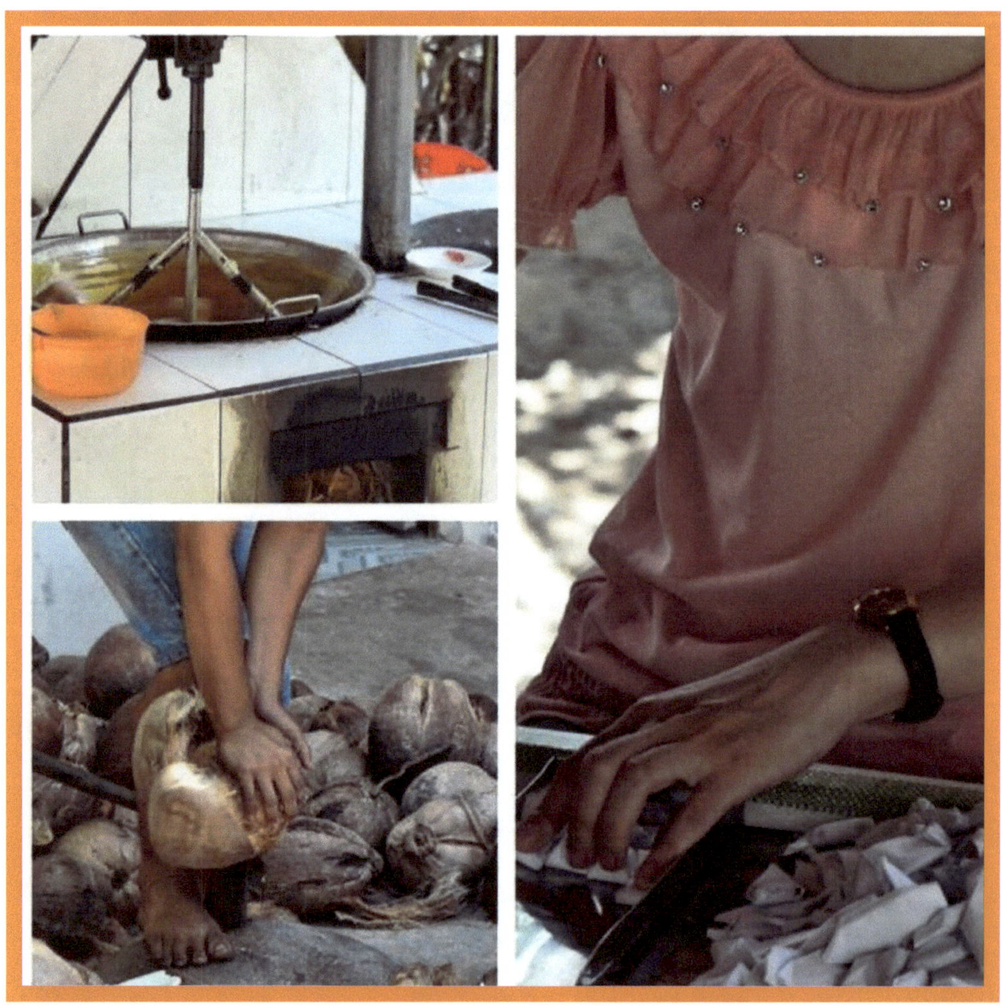

Whenever I walk in areas such as Ben Tre, or any other fruit and produce areas, I must constantly remind myself to look up at the trees. It is always a surprise to see the things that are growing above!

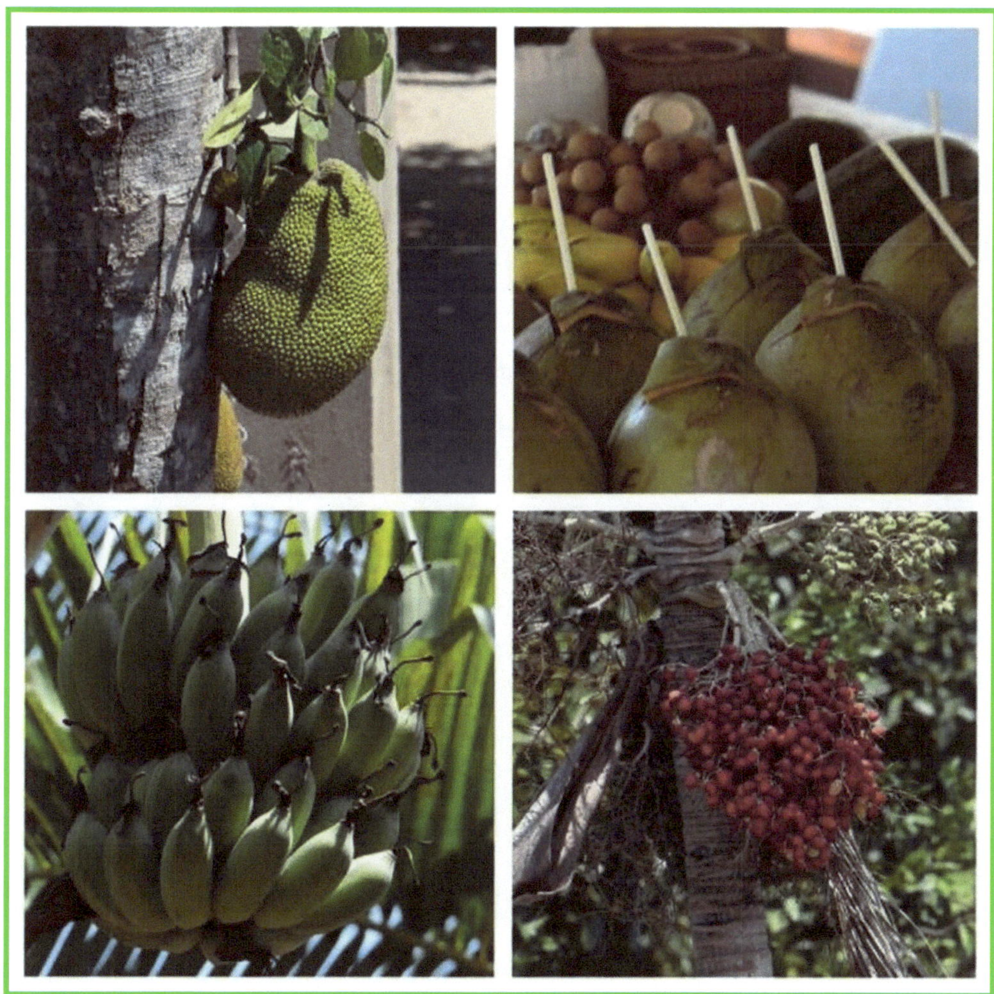

As we left Ben Tre and returned to Saigon, along the Mekong River, we once again marveled at the hard life on the river. As we watched the views of this life roll by, we were reminded of the stark contrast between the modern buildings and small cities along the shore versus the many shacks and watercraft that mysteriously kept floating by. One cannot help but admire the hard work, and sometimes harsh living conditions, on the river.

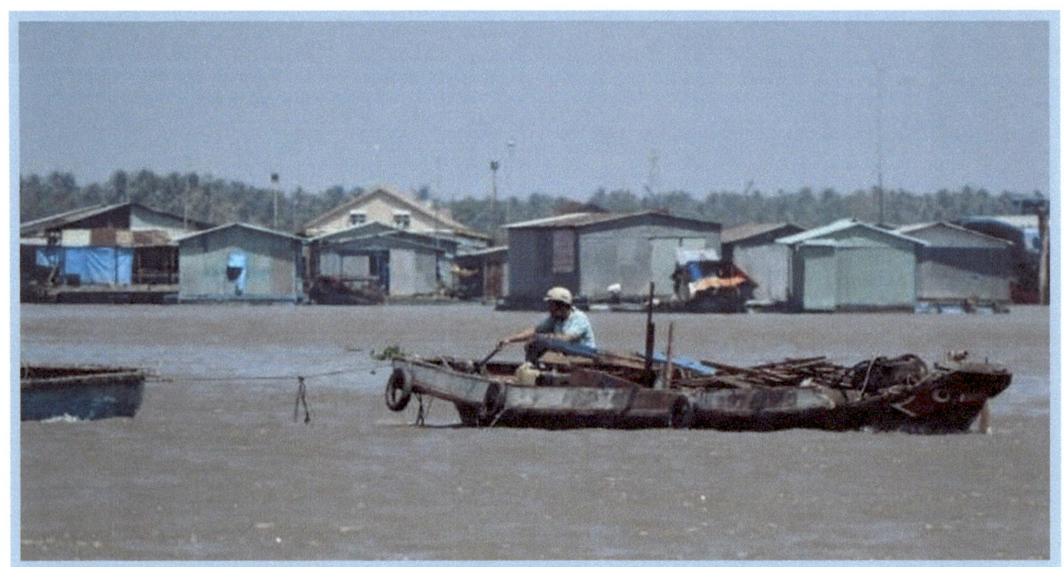

The Rach Mieu Bridge—a cable suspension-type bridge that spans the Tien River—is an example of modern-day Vietnam and has had a great effect on river provinces. Linking two provinces together, the bridge is a source of great pride since it is the first bridge designed and constructed by Vietnamese engineers and construction experts. Ben Tre, its prior access having been mainly by river, is no longer the isolated province it used to be. Progress has come from access provided by this bridge.

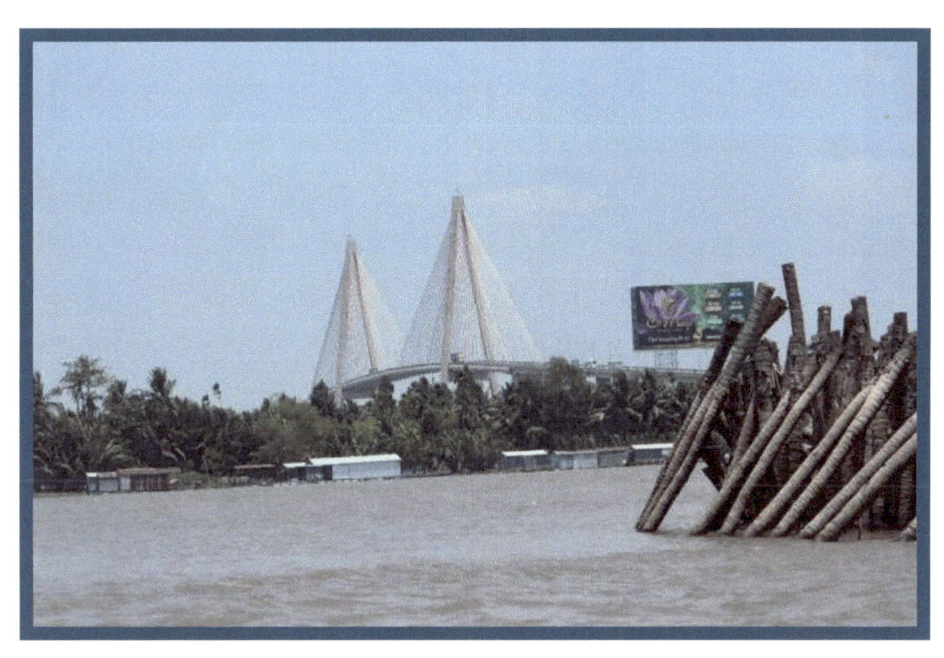

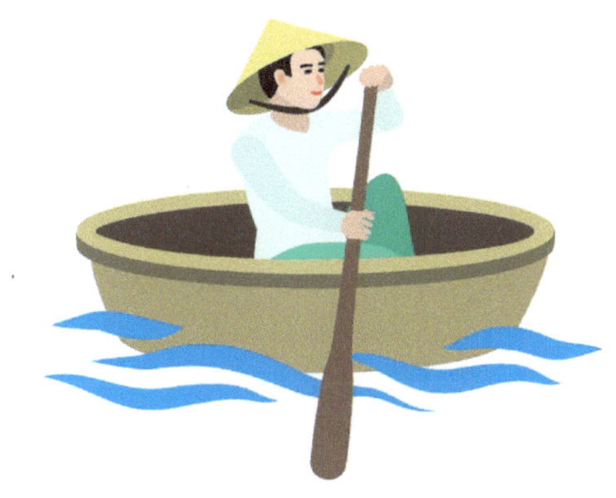

12—In and Around Saigon

Ho Chi Minh City (Saigon) is a huge metropolitan area with 16 different districts and a population exceeding nine million people. Though it may no longer be the "Paris of the Orient" to some, it is a beautiful city to visit, nonetheless. One place I looked forward to seeing was Cholon, the Chinese district. A huge portion of Saigon, the district covers roughly half the land area and has several million Chinese living there. We were told that if you look at the total size of the area, you will see that it is the largest Chinese city outside of China.

Fifty years ago, I visited Cholon on many occasions. I have gone to Cholon for lunch or dinner several times in the past. These meals consisted of a huge bowl of steamed clams in a garlic and white wine sauce, a small baguette of French bread, and a glass of wine, all for little more than a dollar. This blend of French and Vietnamese cooking made for the best meals during my

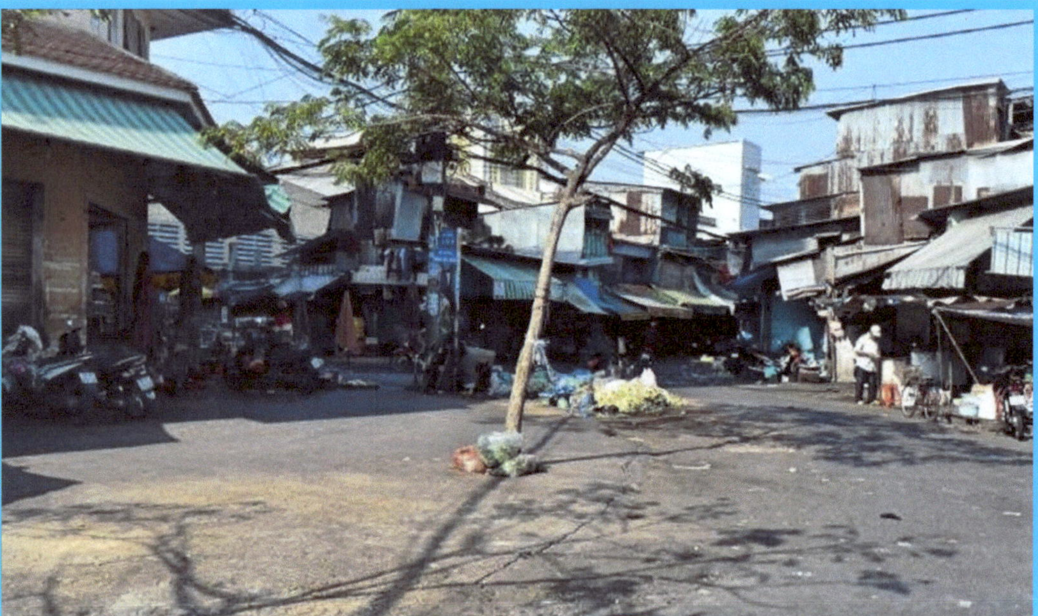

time in Cholon. When the 1968 Tet Offensive occurred and the reality of war was upon us, those meals, along with any trips outside of our compound or work area, ended.

Today, some of these areas still look much the same. Some of the market areas and neighborhoods looked as though they had not changed at all in the 50 years between my visits.

The tour of Cholon did not visit many of the areas I had wanted to see, so I mentioned to our tour guide that I wanted to see more. He arranged a scooter ride for me with someone he trusted who agreed to take me on a tour of today's Cholon or, at least, part of it. I tried to give him an idea of what I had seen 50 years prior, and his tour did not disappoint.

In almost every corner of Cholon, there are alleyways with stalls. These areas are almost identical to what I saw during my first time there. Sometimes the small markets are a photographer's delight.

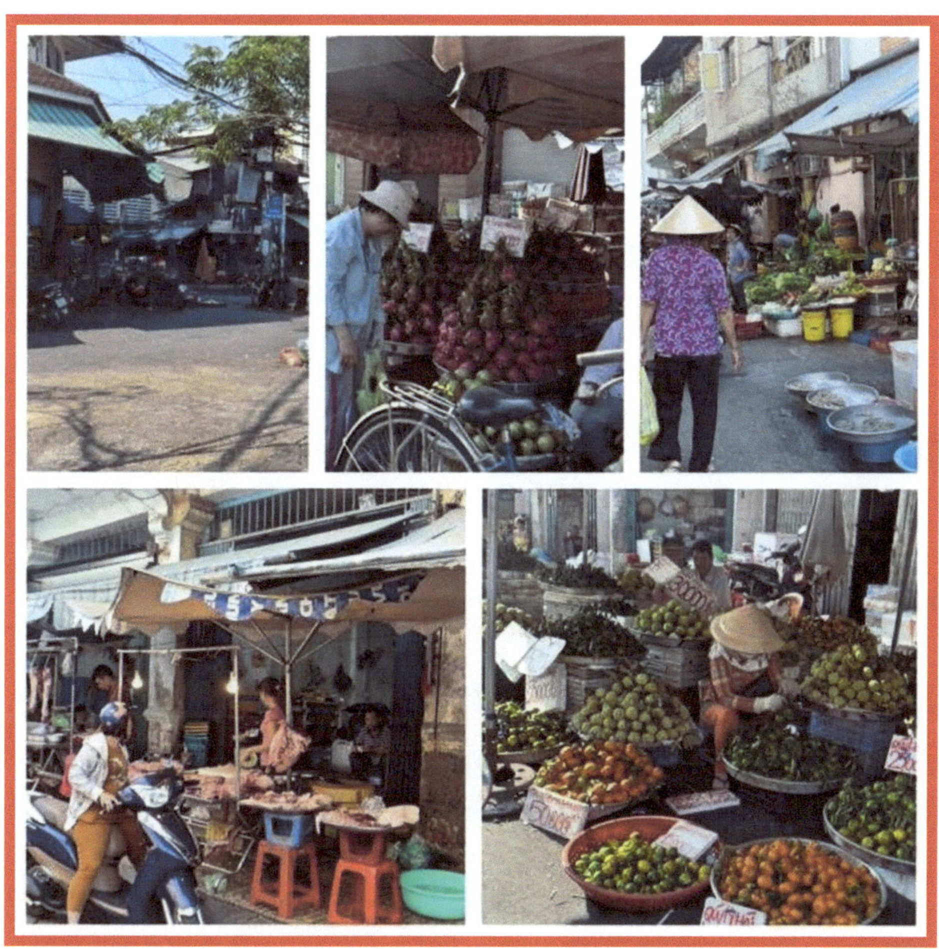

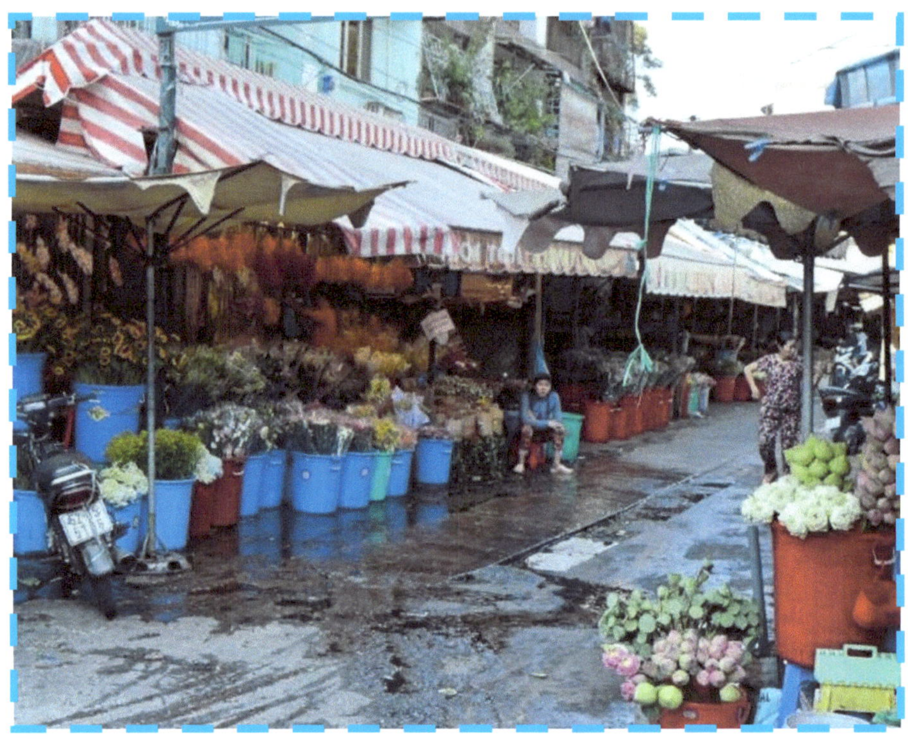

When visiting Cholon, make sure to allow enough time to stop at the Binh Tay Market. Not only is it Cholon's huge, central market, but it is also a major agricultural distribution hub where you will see products from all over the southern sections of Vietnam. A major tourist attraction, its stalls number more than 2,000 selling everything you can—or can't—imagine.

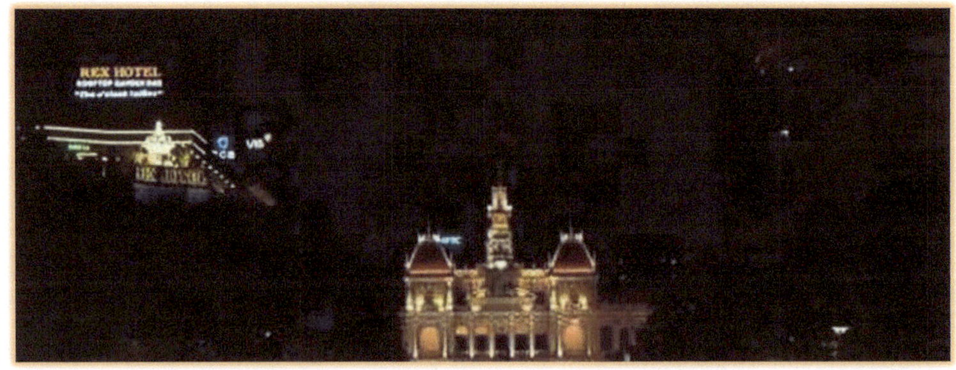

After an extended day in Cholon, we spent the evening in Saigon enjoying all the wonderful nighttime sights the city has to offer. The narrow, little picture of the Rex Hotel is a place of historic significance. This is where the news media received its weekly, and rather overstated, war progress briefings. Members of the press referred to these briefings as "The Friday Follies."

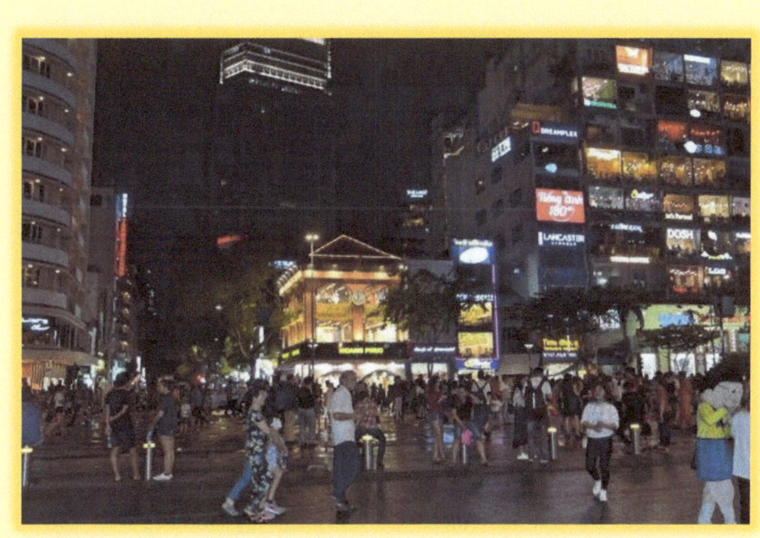

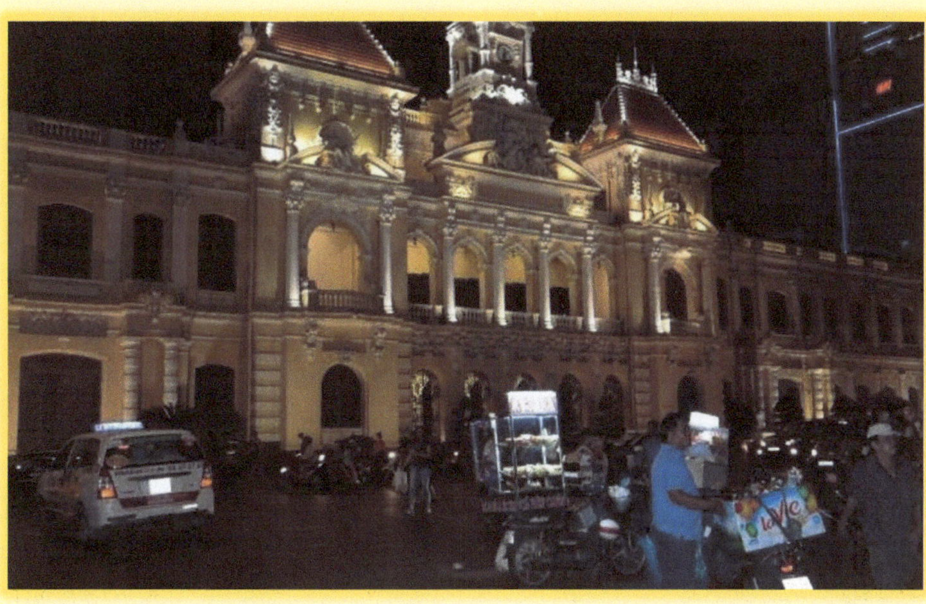

Until 1975, this beautiful building was known as City Hall. Now it serves as a government office that has been renamed "People's Committee" since it is the headquarters for the group of that name. Designed by French architects during the time of the French Indochina government, it is of similar design to Paris' city hall. It was constructed in the early 1900's and took six years to complete. Due to the large crowds, it was difficult for me to get a good picture when I was around the building. You may have to be more patient that I was if you are hoping to snap a photo. In the upper, right corner, this picture shows a contrast be tween old and new and it is quite visual. Despite the heat and humidity, nighttime is special anywhere in Vietnam. Whether in the rural towns and villages, with their characteristic electric lanterns, or in the large cities with tall high rises with colonial-designed, historic buildings, make sure you have lots of storage space in your camera. It will need to be enough to take more pictures than you will ever need.

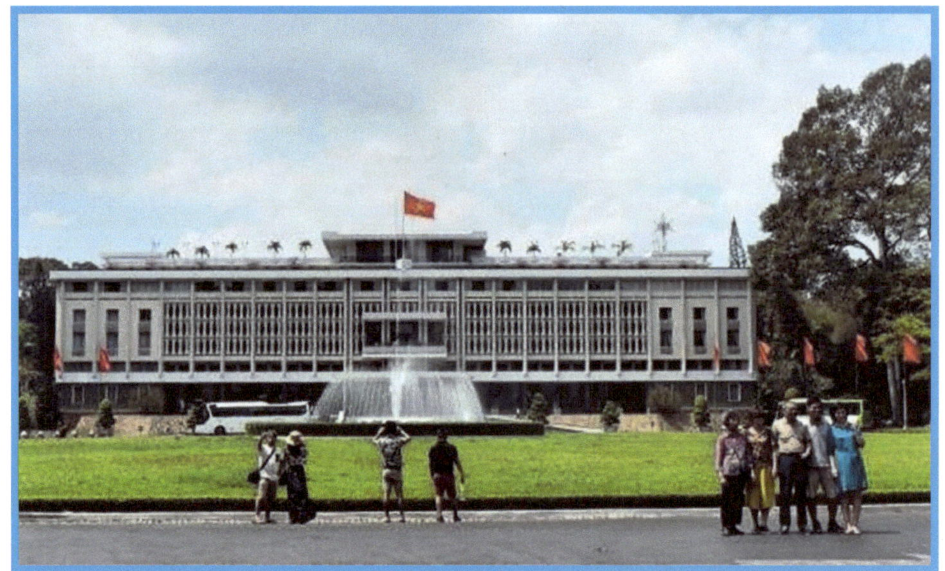

Do not miss seeing this impressive building during the day. I knew it as the Presidential Palace Where the President of South Vietnam lived and worked. The palace's construction was completed a few years be fore my first tour. Today, it looks the same as it did when I walked by it back in 1967. It is now known as "The Reunification Convention Hall." It is a visual setting with a park situated next door and the building framed somewhat by trees. There were always dozens of people from all over the world stopping for a photo.

Close by is the War Remnants Museum. It houses several floors of images, many of which are graphic in detail, along with the stories of the photographers at that time. Since it is from the point of view of the Vietnamese, communist government, some may view it as propaganda. I did not see much to argue with, concerning the horrors of war. One interesting thing we saw was a large photo of a group of American, college-aged, young people protesting the war. In front of the photo stood a group of men around my age getting their pictures taken. We were told they were the same young people from the photo who had been protesting. Although there were scores of pictures like that, I would have liked to have seen the pictures of the protests that occurred in Vietnam during that time.

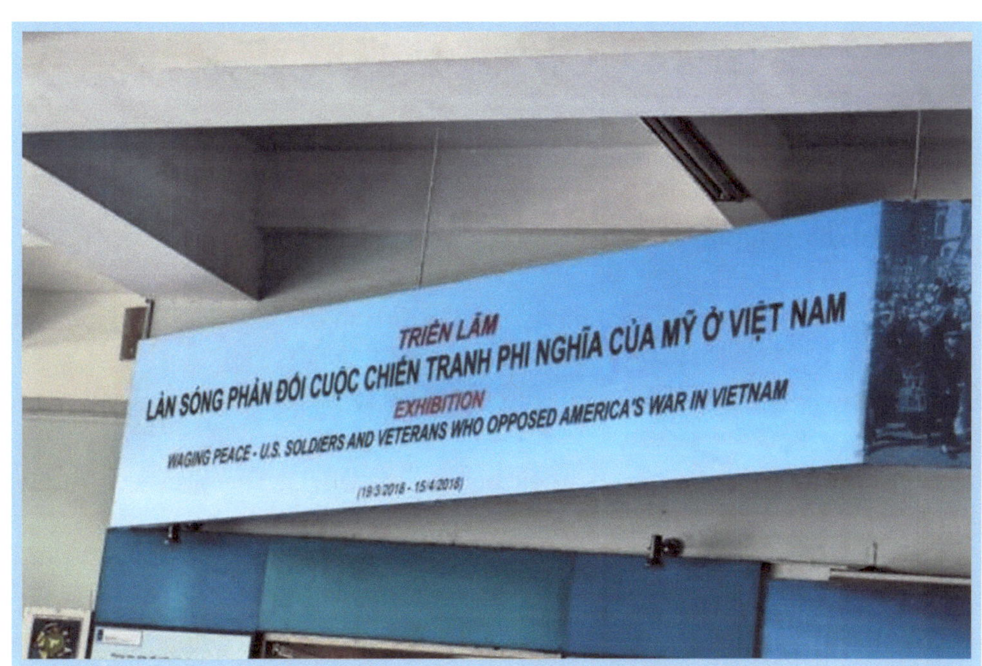

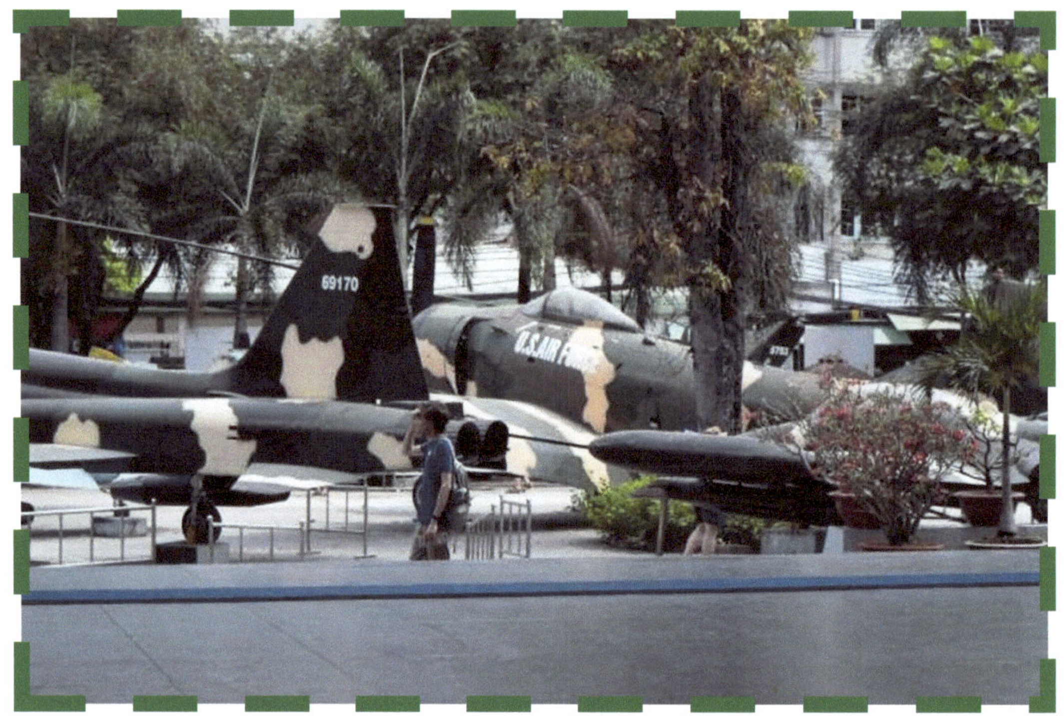

On the grounds of the War Remnant Museum are numerous displays of captured or abandoned weapons that were used or supplied by the US during the war. Though it was not my cup of tea, it was well done and the kids loved it. After all, the war is several generations removed from the very young—it is mostly just a part of their history lesson. Once you have visited the museum, be sure to leave time to see the historic Saigon Central Post Office, another French, colonial-designed structure built in the late 1880s. During my visit, it was still a functional post office. If you find the same is true for you, be sure to send a letter back home! The inside of the post office is just as popular to tour as the outside. When I was there it was crowded both inside and out, so be sure you leave plenty of time. There were even large crowds waiting in line to post their cards and letters.

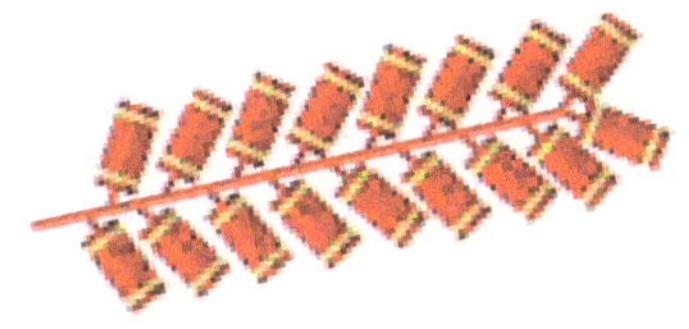

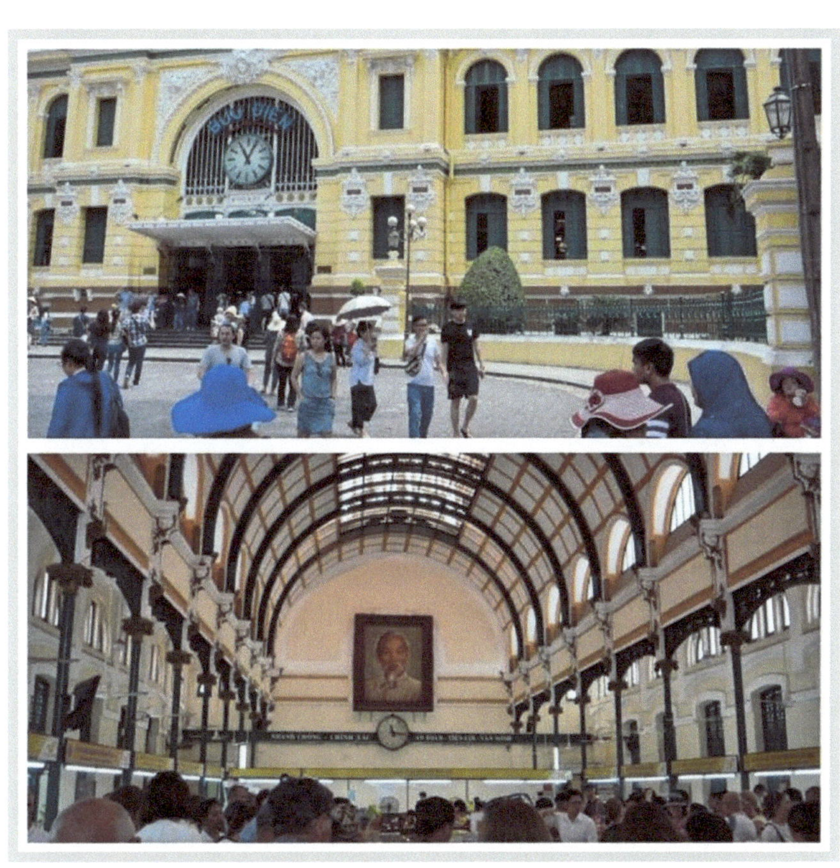

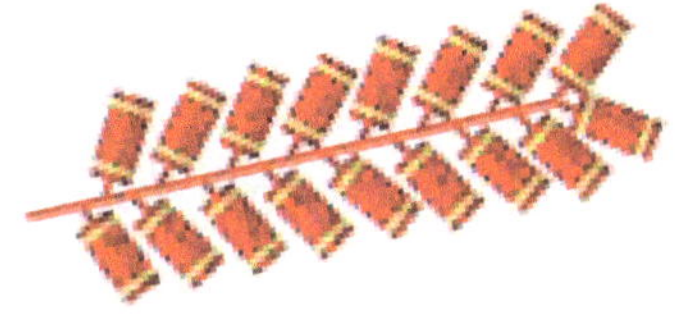

Next to the post office is another French-designed building that is a favorite of photographers from all over the world. This is the famous Notre Dame Cathedral Saigon and is said to be in the top 20 of the world's most majestic and beautiful cathedrals. Construction of the building dates to the 1860-70s and was financed by the French government. Many of the construction materials were shipped from France. When I first saw this in 1967, it was in an undeveloped part of Saigon near the post office and, back then, I was told, it was a ¼ size replica of France's Notre Dame Cathedral.

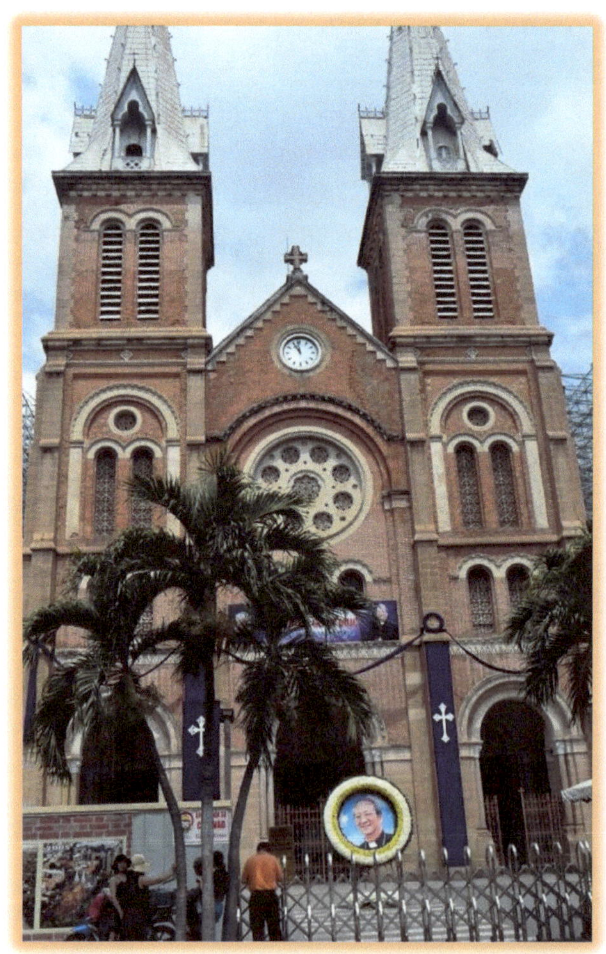

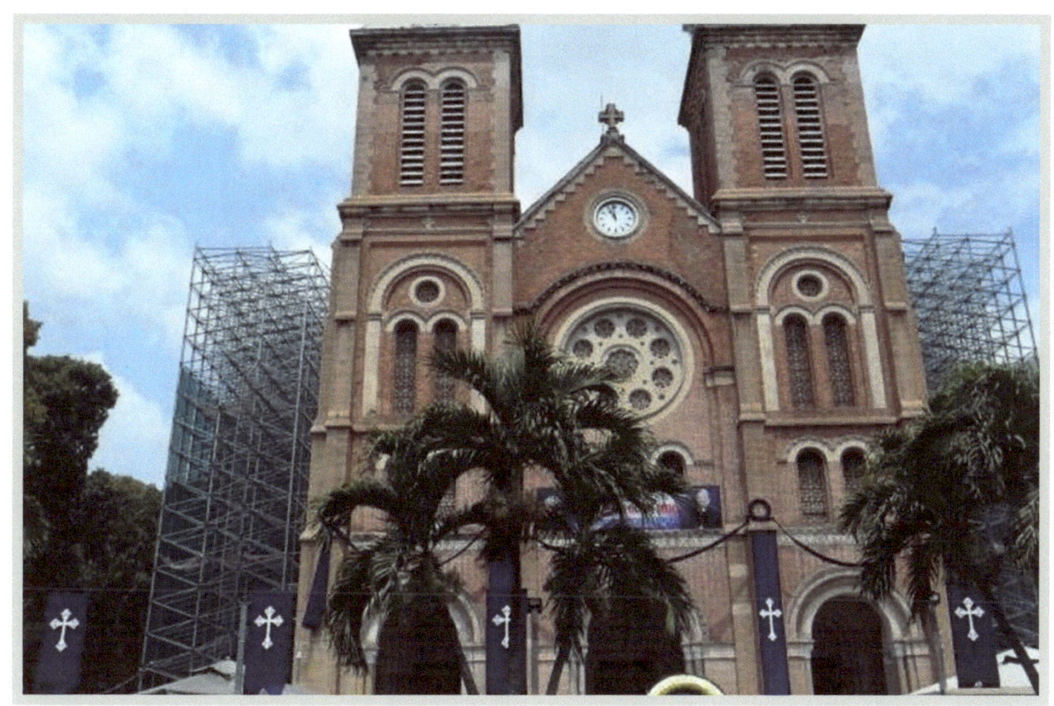

As you can see clearer in the second picture, the Cathedral is under major repair. It is still under repair years later and is currently only around 50% complete as they are working on cleaning walls, replacing the roof, and much more. The estimated time for completion of all renovations and repairs is 2027. Concerning timelines, the current philosophy is to not rush the process. COVID and supply issues contributed to delays. Regardless of its stage of completion, it is still worthwhile to visit this beautiful cathedral.

One thing I liked about wandering the streets of Saigon was the many buildings still in place from the early 1800s, as well as the classic architecture near the start of the 1900s. I had to constantly remind myself to turn and look in all directions so I wouldn't miss a historic, French-designed building like the opera house built in 1898. It is now known as the Municipal Theatre of Ho Chi Minh City.

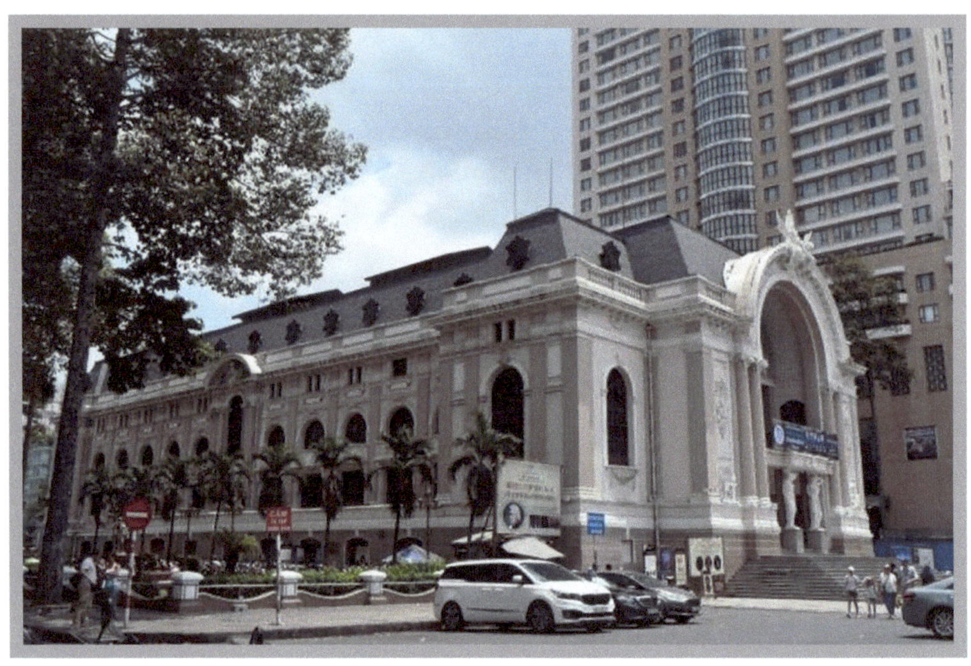

VIETNAM

After visiting areas in the delta, or walking around Cholon and downtown Saigon, you may choose to visit many other interesting places that are a short distance away. One of these is Cu Chi. Though it is a beautiful area, many who remember the war think of it only as the Cu Chi Tunnels—a site our tour, like most tours, visited. For many Veterans, this is probably not something they will relish seeing. But for historians, young people, or anyone else interested in seeing what the Viet Cong had to do to, from their perspective, to win the war, it is worthwhile. I did not know that the tunnels extended over 250 kilometers, and construction was originally started by the Viet Minh, aiding their eventual defeat of the French. Those early tunnels were built to connect one family to another—one hamlet to another—and gradually expanded to have hidden spaces for storage, barracks, hospitals, and escape routes.

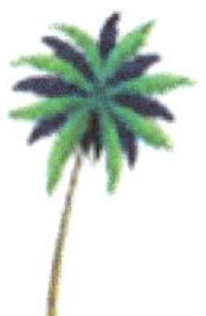
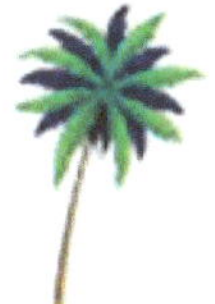
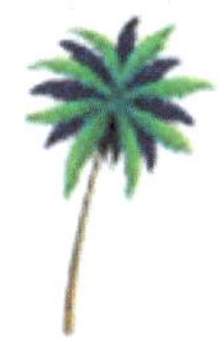

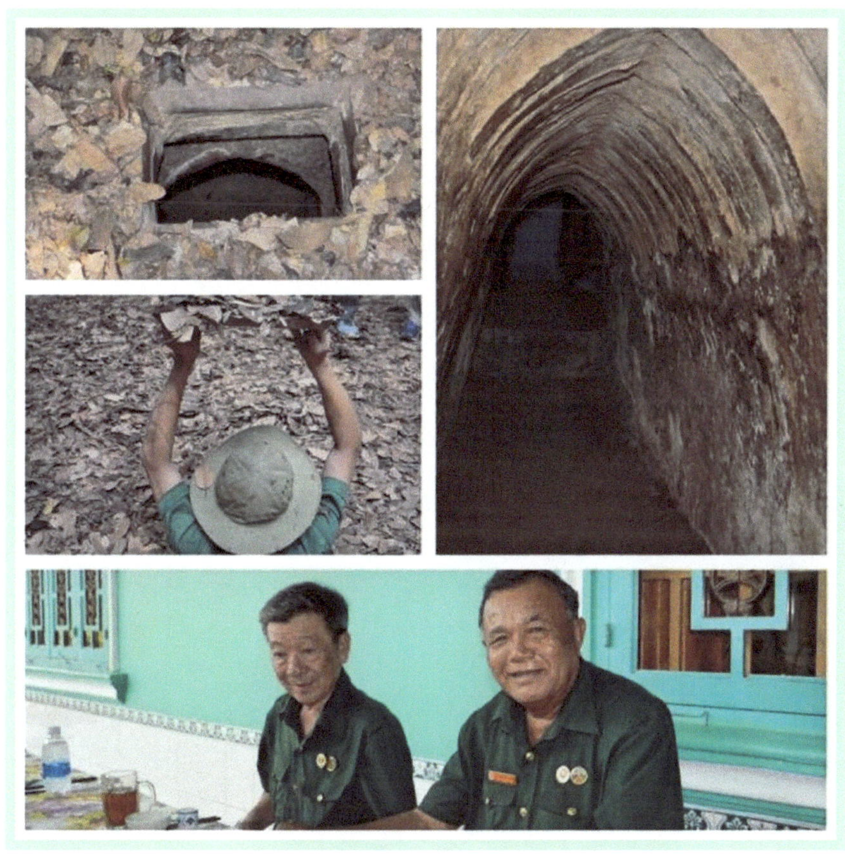

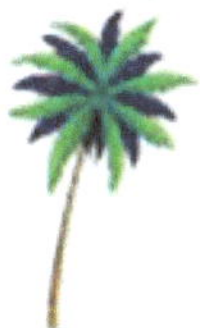
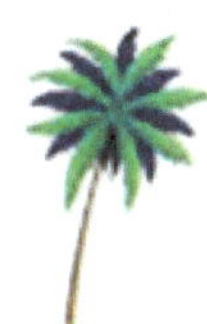
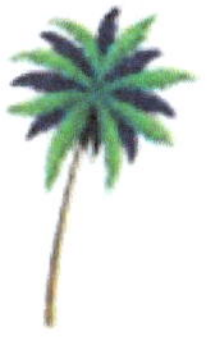

The tunnels that are available for visitors to crawl through have been enlarged for more headroom. I went in only a little way and, even though it had been enlarged, it was not a comfortable experience. If you look closely at the picture of that tunnel, you can see the change of color where the height was increased. That also gives you an idea of how much lower it used to be.

After a visit to the tunnel site, we had lunch at the home of a Viet Cong officer along with a fellow officer. They told us they spend almost all their spare time trying to get health and other benefits for Viet Cong veterans. After reunification, the North Vietnamese soldiers received benefits, but the Viet Cong vets did not.

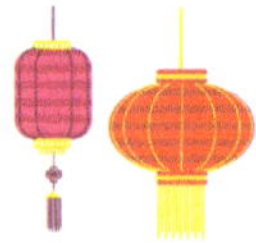

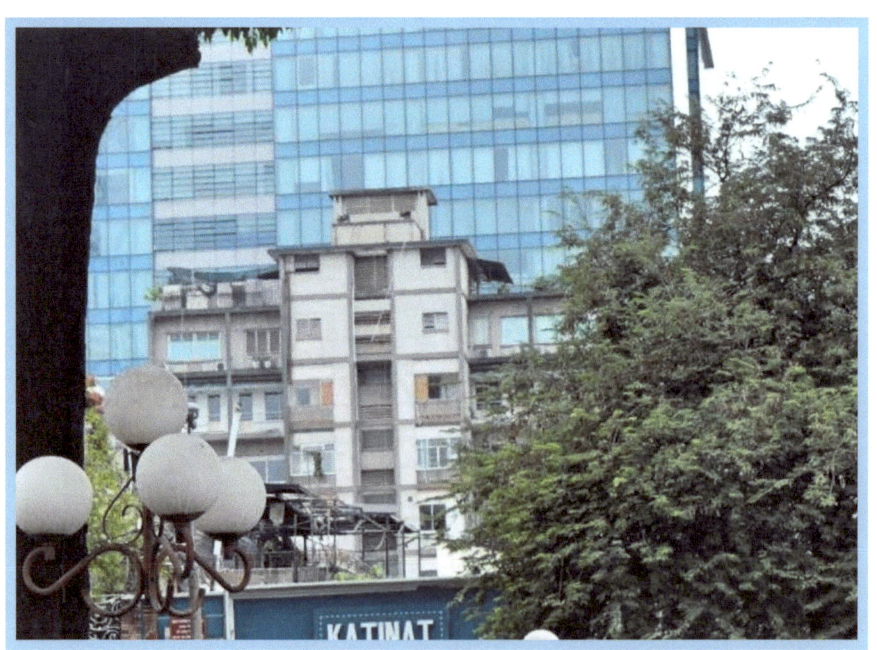

I am going to end my golden journey back to Vietnam with this picture, which may seem rather odd to many. The building was featured in one of the most iconic news photos seen around the world.

It was taken in 1975, by Dutch photographer and journalist, Hubert van Es, hours before the fall of Saigon. In the photo, there is a helicopter on the roof with a ladder leading from below. The president, his family, and other officials were to be evacuated. The ladder is filled with people on every rung, and only those cleared would be evacuated. Early news reports stated it was the US Embassy when, in fact, it was the Pittman Apartment Building—a CIA safe house. When I took my photo, we were told it was going to be torn down. It has been under tear-down status on many occasions. Currently, it is holding a small rooftop café.

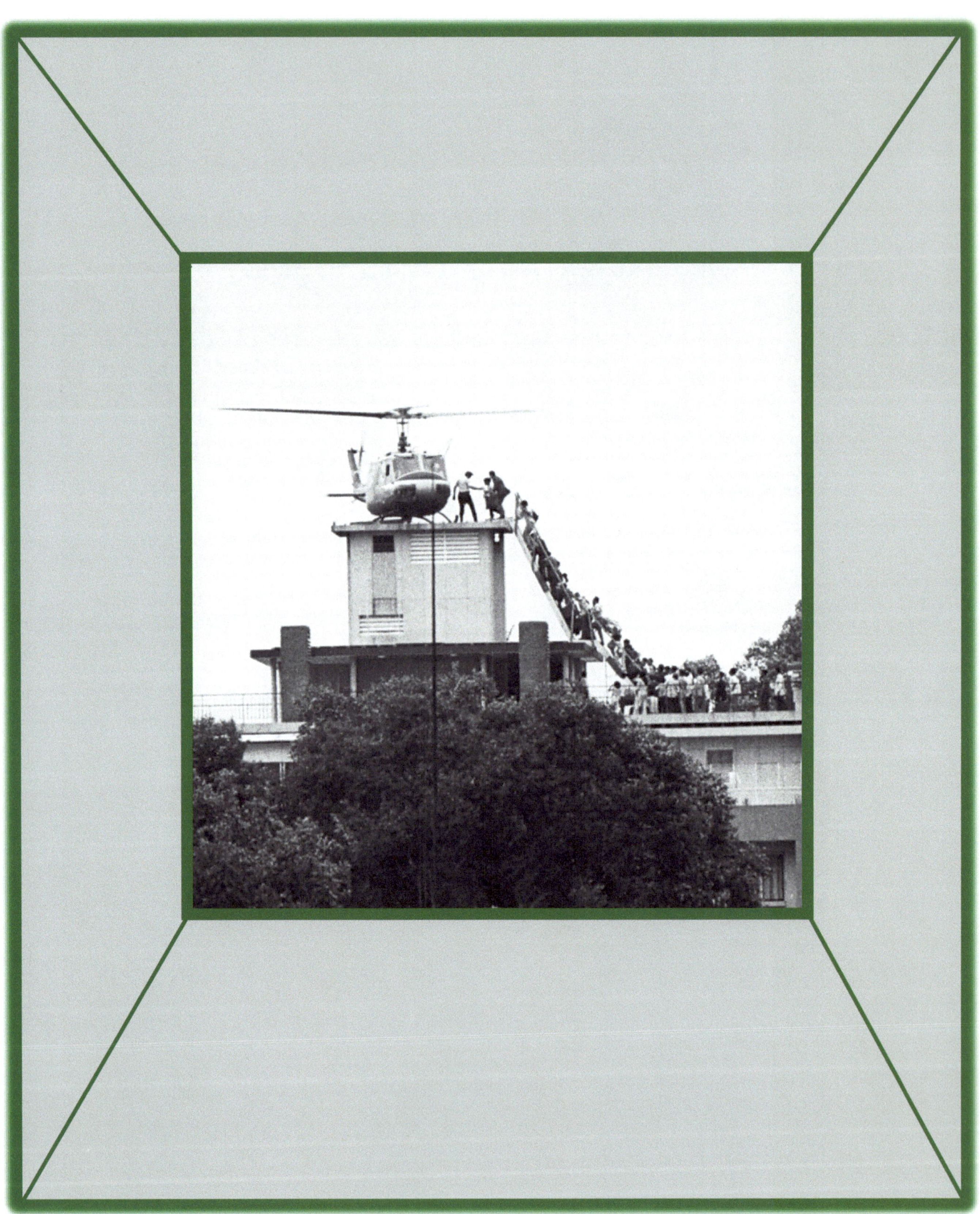

And that is the end of my journey. I hope you enjoyed it. There is much more to see than what I have covered. If you would like more information about my hotels, the tour company I used, or anything else, you may email me using my first and last name together at Gmail.

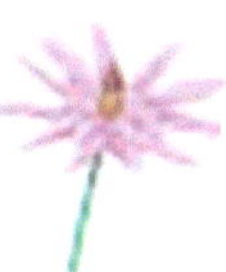

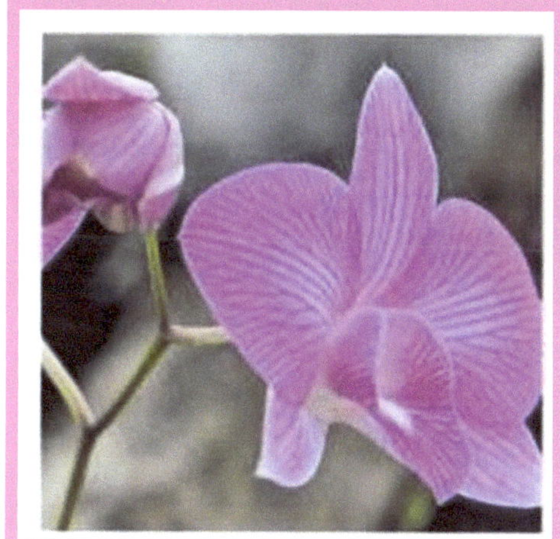

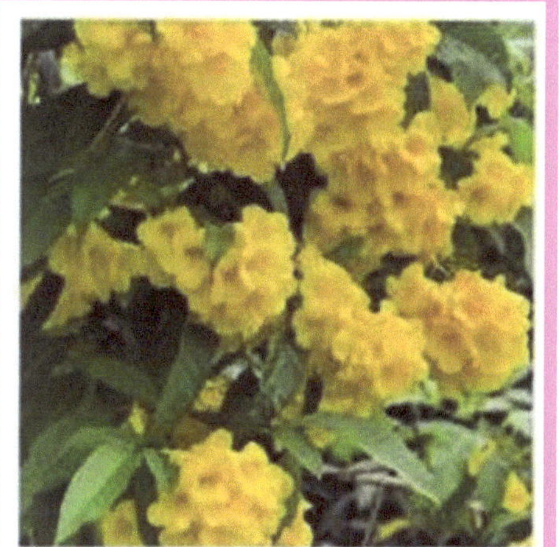

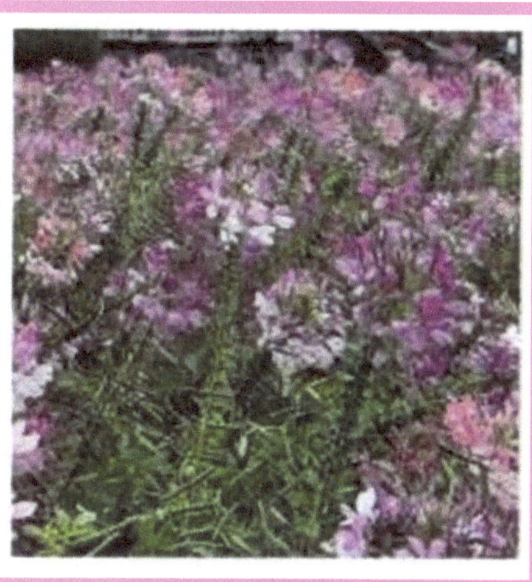

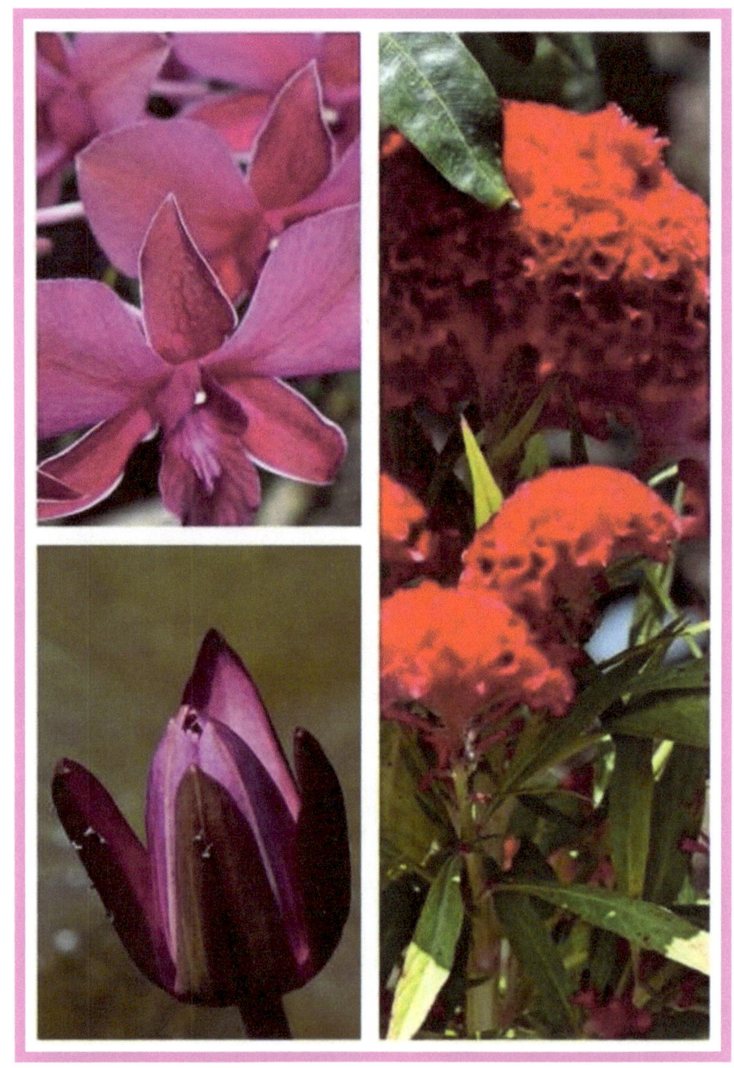

Author Ken Palmrose

Mr. Palmrose was born and raised in Clatsop County Oregon in the Seaside-Astoria area. He graduated from Seaside High School and later from Clatsop Community College with an Associates Degree in Forestry Technology. He was drafted into the Army and then trained as an imagery interpreter at Ft. Holabird, MD Military Intelligence School. He served in Vietnam for parts of 1967 and 1968, including during the infamous Tet offensive. For many years during his 36-year Forest Service career, he was a writer and editor, and later a contributing editor for an extensive Arizona wildfire story titled "The Monster Reared His Ugly Head." Mr. Palmrose wrote numerous news and web stories, special feature articles and additionally he continued learning to be an accomplished photographer. He has travelled to over 25 countries around the world. As a 75-year-old first time published author from Meridian, Idaho, he was thrilled to have his very first novel published and now has more to write. He recently completed his second novel, a revision of the first, which is now doubled in length. In 2023, he had a unique collection of his first ever free-verse poetry published along with some photos he has taken during his travels.

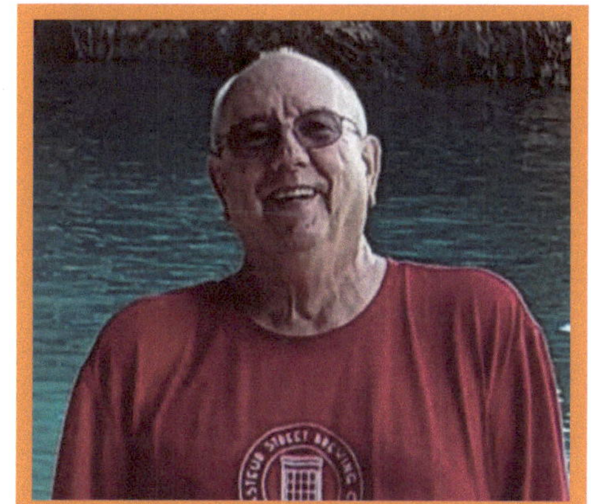

www.ingramcontent.com/pod-product-compliance
Lightning Source LLC
LaVergne TN
LVHW070216110826
845147LV00003B/589
9798990582057